A Critical Examination of Socialism

By William Hurrell Mallock

I0410959

PREFACE

The Civic Federation of New York, an influential body which aims, in various ways, at harmonising apparently divergent industrial interests in America, having decided on supplementing its other activities by a campaign of political and economic education, invited me, at the beginning of the year 1907, to initiate a scientific discussion of socialism in a series of lectures or speeches, to be delivered under the auspices of certain of the great Universities in the United States. This invitation I accepted, but, the project being a new one, some difficulty arose as to the manner in which it might best be carried out--whether the speeches or lectures should in each case be new, dealing with some fresh aspect of the subject, or whether they should be arranged in a single series to be repeated without substantial alteration in each of the cities visited by me. The latter plan was ultimately adopted, as tending to render the discussion of the subject more generally comprehensible to each local audience. A series of five lectures, substantially the same, was accordingly delivered by me in New York, Cambridge, Chicago, Philadelphia, and Baltimore. But whilst this plan secured continuity of treatment, it secured it at the expense of comprehensiveness. Certain important points had to be passed over. In the present volume the substance of the original lectures has been entirely rearranged and rewritten, and more than half the matter is new. Even in the present volume, however, it has been impossible to treat the subject otherwise than in a general way. At almost every point a really complete discussion would necessitate a much fuller analysis of facts than it has been practicable to give here. Arguments here necessarily confined to a few pages or to a chapter, would each, for their complete elucidation, require a separate monograph. Most readers, however, will be able to supply much of what is missing, by the light of their own common sense; and general arguments, in which, as in block plans of buildings, many details are suppressed, have for practical purposes the great advantage of being generally and easily intelligible, whereas, if stated in fuller and more complex form, they might confuse rather than enlighten a large number of readers.

The fact that the fundamental arguments of this volume were disseminated throughout the United States, not only at the meetings addressed, but also in all the leading newspapers, has had the valuable result, by means of the mass of criticisms which they elicited, of illustrating the manner in which socialists attempt to meet them; and has enabled me to revise, with a view to farther clearness, certain passages which were intentionally or unintentionally misunderstood, and also to emphasise the curious confusions of thought into which various critics have been driven in their efforts to controvert or get round them. I may specially mention a small volume by Mr. G. Wilshire of New York--a leading publisher and disseminator of socialistic literature-- which was devoted to examining my own arguments seriatim. To the principal criticisms of this writer allusions will be found in the following pages. Most of my socialistic opponents (though to this rule there were amusing exceptions) wrote, according to their varying degrees of intelligence and education, with remarkable candour, and also with great courtesy. Mr. Wilshire, in particular, whilst seeking to refute my arguments as a whole, admitted the force of many of them; and did his best to state them all fairly.

The contentions, and even the phraseology of socialists are in all countries (with the possible exception of Russia) identical. All are vitiated by the same distinctive errors, and it is indifferent whether, for purposes of detail criticism, we go to speakers and writers in this country or America. Except for the correction of a few verbal errors which have escaped my notice in the American edition, and which obscure the meaning of perhaps four or five sentences, for the introduction of a few additional notes, and for the translation of dollars and cents into pounds and shillings, the English and the American editions are the same.

W. H. M.

January, 1908.

CONTENTS

CHAPTER I

THE HISTORICAL BEGINNING OF SOCIALISM AS AN OSTENSIBLY SCIENTIFIC THEORY

Socialism an unrealised theory. In order to discuss it, it must be defined.

Being of no general interest except as a nucleus of some general movement, we must identify it as a theory which has united large numbers of men in a common demand for change.

As the definite theoretical nucleus of a party or movement, socialism dates from the middle of the nineteenth century, when it was erected into a formal system by Karl Marx.

We must begin our examination of it by taking it in this, its earliest, systematic form.

CHAPTER II

THE THEORY OF MARX AND THE EARLIER SOCIALISTS SUMMARISED

The doctrine of Marx that all wealth is produced by labour.

His recognition that the possibilities of distribution rest on the facts of production.

His theory of labour as the sole producer of wealth avowedly derived from Ricardo's theory of value.

His theory of capital as consisting of implements of production, which are embodiments of past labour, and his theory of modern capitalism as representing nothing but a gradual abstraction by a wholly unproductive class, of these implements from the men who made them, and who alone contribute anything to their present productive use.

His theory that wages could never rise, but must, under capitalism, sink all over the world to the amount which would just keep the labourers from starvation, when, driven by necessity, they will rebel, and, repossessing themselves of their own implements, will be rich forever afterwards by using them for their own benefit.

CHAPTER III

THE ROOT ERROR OF THE MARXIAN THEORY. ITS OMISSION OF DIRECTIVE ABILITY. ABILITY AND LABOUR DEFINED

The theory of Marx analysed. It is true as applied to primitive communities, where the amount of wealth produced is very small, but it utterly fails to account for the increased wealth of the modern world.

Labour, as Marx conceived of it, can indeed increase in productivity in two ways, but to a small degree only, neither of which explains the vast increase of wealth during the past hundred and fifty years.

The cause of this is the development of a class which, not labouring itself, concentrates exceptional knowledge and energy on the task of directing the labour of others, as an author does when, by means of his manuscript, he directs the labour of compositors.

Formal definition of the parts played respectively by the faculties of the labouring and those of the directing classes.

CHAPTER IV

THE ERRORS OF MARX, CONTINUED. CAPITAL AS THE IMPLEMENT OF ABILITY

Two kinds of human effort being thus involved in modern production, it is necessary for all purposes of intelligible discussion to distinguish them by different names.

The word "labour" being appropriated by common custom to the manual task-work of the majority, some other technical word must be found to designate the directive faculties as applied to productive industry. The word here chosen, in default of a better, is "ability."

Ability, then, being the faculty which directs labour, by what means does it give effect to its directions?

It gives effect to its directions by means of its control of capital, in the form of wage-capital.

Ability, using wage-capital as its implement of direction, gives rise to fixed capital, in the form of the elaborate implements of modern production, which are the material embodiments of the knowledge, ingenuity, and energy of the highest minds.

CHAPTER V

REPUDIATION OF MARX BY MODERN SOCIALISTS. THEIR RECOGNITION OF DIRECTIVE ABILITY

The more educated socialists of to-day, when the matter is put plainly before them, admit that the argument of the preceding chapters is correct, and repudiate the doctrine of Marx that "labour" is the sole producer.

Examples of this admission on the part of American socialists.

The socialism of Marx, however, still remains the socialism of the more ignorant classes, and also of the popular agitator.

It is, moreover, still used as an instrument of agitation by many who personally repudiate it. The case of Mr. Hillquit.

The doctrine of Marx, therefore, still requires exposure.

Further, it is necessary to understand this earlier form of socialistic theory in order to understand the later.

CHAPTER VI

REPUDIATION OF MARX BY MODERN SOCIALISTS, CONTINUED. THEIR RECOGNITION OF CAPITAL AS THE IMPLEMENT OF DIRECTIVE ABILITY. THEIR NEW POSITION, AND THEIR NEW THEORETICAL DIFFICULTIES

The more educated socialists of to-day, besides virtually accepting the argument of the preceding chapters with regard to labour, virtually accept the argument set forth in them with regard to capital.

Mr. Sidney Webb, for example, recognises it as an implement of direction, the only alternative to which is a system of legal coercion.

Other socialists advocate the continued use of wage-capital as the implement of direction, but they imagine that the situation would be radically changed by making the "state" the sole capitalist.

But the "state," as some of them are beginning to realise, would be merely the private men of ability--the existing employers--turned into state officials, and deprived of most of their present inducements to exert themselves.

A socialistic state theoretically could always command labour, for labour can be exacted by force; but the exercise of ability must be voluntary, and can only be secured by a system of adequate rewards and inducements.

Two problems with which modern socialism is confronted: How would it test its able men so as to select the best of them for places of power? What rewards could it offer them which would induce them systematically to develop, and be willing to exercise, their exceptional faculties?

CHAPTER VII

PROXIMATE DIFFICULTIES. ABLE MEN AS A CORPORATION OF STATE OFFICIALS

How are the men fittest for posts of industrial power to be selected from the less fit?

This problem solved automatically by the existing system of private and separate capitals.

The fusion of all private capitals into a single state capital would make this solution impossible, and would provide no other. The only machinery by which the more efficient directors of labour could be discriminated from the less efficient would be broken. Case of the London County Council's steamboats.

Two forms which the industrial state under socialism might conceivably take: The official directors of industry might be either an autocratic bureaucracy, or they might else be subject to elected politicians representing the knowledge and opinions prevalent among the majority.

Estimate of the results which would arise in the former case. Illustrations from actual bureaucratic enterprise.

Estimate of the results which would arise in the latter case. The state, as representing the average opinion of the masses, brought to bear on scientific industrial enterprise. Illustrations.

The state as sole printer and publisher. State capitalism would destroy the machinery of industrial progress just as it would destroy the machinery by which thought and knowledge develop.

But behind the question of whether socialism could provide ability with the conditions or the machinery requisite for its exercise is the question of whether it could provide it with any adequate stimulus.

CHAPTER VIII

THE ULTIMATE DIFFICULTY. SPECULATIVE ATTEMPTS TO MINIMISE IT

Mr. Sidney Webb, and most modern socialists of the higher kind, recognise that this problem of motive underlies all others.

They approach it indirectly by sociological arguments borrowed from other philosophers, and directly by a psychology peculiar to themselves.

The sociological arguments by which socialists seek to minimise the claims of the able man.

These founded on a specific confusion of thought, which vitiated the evolutionary sociology of that second half of the nineteenth century. Illustrations from Herbert Spencer, Macaulay, Mr. Kidd, and recent socialists.

The confusion in question a confusion between speculative truth and practical.

The individual importance of the able man, untouched by the speculative conclusions of the sociological evolutionists, as may be seen by the examples adduced in a contrary sense by Herbert Spencer. This is partially perceived by Spencer himself. Illustrations from his works.

Ludicrous attempts, on the part of socialistic writers, to apply the speculative generalisations of sociology to the practical position of individual men.

The climax of absurdity reached by Mr. Sidney Webb.

CHAPTER IX

THE ULTIMATE DIFFICULTY, CONTINUED. ABILITY AND INDIVIDUAL MOTIVE

The individual motives of the able man as dealt with directly by modern socialists.

They abandon their sociological ineptitudes altogether, and betake themselves to a psychology which they declare to be scientific, but which is based on no analysis of facts, and consists really of loose assumptions and false analogies.

Their treatment of the motives of the artist, the thinker, the religious enthusiast, and the soldier.

Their unscientific treatment of the soldier's motive, and their fantastic proposal based on it to transfer this motive from the domain of war to that of industry.

The socialists as their own critics when they denounce the actual motives of the able man as he is and as they say he always has been. They attack the typically able man of all periods as a monster of congenital selfishness, and it is men of this special type whom they propose to transform suddenly into monsters of self-abnegation.

Their want of faith in the efficacy of their own moral suasion and their proposal to supplement this by the ballot.

CHAPTER X

INDIVIDUAL MOTIVE AND DEMOCRACY

Exaggerated powers ascribed to democracy by inaccurate thinkers.

An example from an essay by a recent philosophic thinker, with special reference to the rewards of exceptional ability.

This writer maintains that the money rewards of ability can be determined by the opinion of the majority expressing itself through votes and statutes.

The writer's typical error. A governing body might enact any laws, but they would not be obeyed unless consonant with human nature.

Laws are obliged to conform to the propensities of human nature which it is their office to regulate.

Elaborate but unconscious admission of this fact by the writer here quoted himself.

The power of democracy in the economic sphere, its magnitude and its limits. The demands of the minority a counterpart of those of the majority.

The demand of the great wealth-producer mainly a demand for power.

Testimony of a well-known socialist to the impossibility of altering the character of individual demand by outside influence.

CHAPTER XI

CHRISTIAN SOCIALISM AS A SUBSTITUTE FOR SECULAR DEMOCRACY

The meaning of Christian socialism, as restated to-day by a typical writer.

His just criticism of the fallacy underlying modern ideas of democracy. The impossibility of equalising unequal men by political means.

Christian socialism teaches, he says, that the abler men should make themselves equal to ordinary men by surrendering to them the products of their own ability, or else by abstaining from its exercise.

The author's ignorance of the nature of the modern industrial process. His idea of steel.

He confuses the production of wealth on a great scale with the acquisition of wealth when produced.

The only really productive ability which he distinctly recognises is that of the speculative inventor.

He declares that inventors never wish to profit personally by their inventions. Let the great capitalists, he says, who merely monopolise inventions, imitate the self-abnegation of the inventors, and Christian socialism will become a fact.

The confusion which reigns in the minds of sentimentalists like the author here quoted. Their inability to see complex facts and principles, in their connected integrity, as they are. Such persons herein similar to devisers of perpetual motions and systems for defeating the laws of chance at a roulette-table.

All logical socialistic conclusions drawn from premises in which some vital truth or principle is omitted. Omission in the premises of the earlier socialists. Corresponding omission in the premises of the socialists of to-day.

Origin of the confusion of thought characteristic of Christian as of all other socialists. Temperamental inability to understand the complexities of economic life. This inability further evidenced by the fact that, with few exceptions, socialists themselves are absolutely incompetent as producers. Certain popular contentions with regard to modern economic life, urged by socialists, but not peculiar to socialism, still remain to be considered in the following chapters.

CHAPTER XII

THE JUST REWARD OF LABOUR AS ESTIMATED BY ITS ACTUAL PRODUCTS

Modern socialists admit that of the wealth produced to-day labour does not produce the whole, but that some part is produced by directive ability. But they contend that labour produces more than it gets. We can only ascertain if such an assertion is correct by discovering how to estimate with some precision the amount produced by labour and ability respectively.

But since for the production of the total product labour and ability are both alike necessary, how can we say that any special proportion of it is produced by one or the other?

J.S. Mill's answer to this question.

The profound error of Mill's argument.

Practically so much of any effect is due to any one of its causes as would be absent from this effect were the cause in question taken away. Illustrations.

Labour itself produces as much as it would produce were there no ability to direct it.

The argument which might be drawn from the case of a community in which there was no labour.

Such an argument illusory; for a community in which there was no labour would be impossible; but the paralysis of ability, or its practical non-existence possible.

Practical reasoning of all kinds always confines itself to the contemplation of possibilities. Illustrations.

Restatement of proposition as to the amount of the product of labour.

The product of ability only partially described by assimilating it to rent.

Ability produces everything which would not be produced if its operation were hampered or suspended.

Increased reward of labour in Great Britain since the year 1800. The reward now received by labour far in excess of what labour itself produces.

In capitalistic countries generally labour gets, not less, but far more than its due, if its due is to be measured by its own products.

It is necessary to remember this; but its due is not to be measured exclusively by its own products.

As will be seen in the concluding chapter.

CHAPTER XIII

INTEREST AND ABSTRACT JUSTICE

The proposal to confiscate interest for the public benefit, on the ground that it is income unconnected with any corresponding effort.

Is the proposal practicable? Is it defensible on grounds of abstract justice?

The abstract moral argument plays a large part in the discussion.

It assumes that a man has a moral right to what he produces, interest being here contrasted with this, as a something which he does not produce.

Defects of this argument. It ignores the element of time. Some forms of effort are productive long after the effort itself has ceased.

For examples, royalties on an acted play. Such royalties herein typical of interest generally.

Industrial interest as a product of the forces of organic nature. Henry George's defence of interest as having this origin.

His argument true, but imperfect. His superficial criticism of Bastiat.

Nature works through machine-capital just as truly as it does in agriculture.

Machines are natural forces captured by men of genius, and set to work for the benefit of human beings.

Interest on machine-capital is part of an extra product which nature is made to yield by those men who are exceptionally capable of controlling her.

By capturing natural forces, one man of genius may add more to the wealth of the world in a year than an ordinary man could add to it in a hundred lifetimes.

The claim of any such man on the products of his genius is limited by a variety of circumstances; but, as a mere matter of abstract justice, the whole of it belongs to him.

Abstract justice, however, in a case like this, gives us no practical guidance, until we interpret it in connection with concrete facts, and translate the just into terms of the practicable.

CHAPTER XIV

THE SOCIALISTIC ATTACK ON INTEREST AND THE NATURE OF ITS SEVERAL ERRORS

The practical outcome of the moral attack on interest is logically an attack on bequest.

Modern socialism would logically allow a man to inherit accumulations, and to spend the principal, but not to receive interest on his money as an investment.

What would be the result if all who inherited capital spent it as income, instead of living on the interest of it?

Two typical illustrations of these ways of treating capital.

The ultimate difference between the two results.

What the treatment of capital as income would mean, if the practice were made universal. It would mean the gradual loss of all the added productive forces with which individual genius has enriched the world.

Practical condemnation of proposed attack on interest.

Another aspect of the matter.

Those who attack interest, as distinct from other kinds of money-reward, admit that the possession of wealth is necessary as a stimulus to production.

But the possession of wealth is desired mainly for its social results far more than for its purely individual results.

Interest as connected with the sustentation of a certain mode of social life.

Further consideration of the manner in which those who attack interest ignore the element of time, and contemplate the present moment only.

The economic functions of a class which is not, at a given moment, economically productive.

Systematic failure of those who attack interest to consider society as a whole, continually emerging from the past, and dependent for its various energies on the prospects of the future.

Consequent futility of the general attack on interest, though interest in certain cases may be justly subjected to special but not exaggerated burdens.

CHAPTER XV

EQUALITY OF OPPORTUNITY

Equality of opportunity, as an abstract demand, is in an abstract sense just; but it changes its character when applied to a world of unequal individuals.

Equality of opportunity in the human race-course. To multiply competitors is to multiply failures.

Educational opportunity. Unequal students soon make opportunities unequal.

Opportunity in industrial life. Socialistic promises of equal industrial opportunities for all. Each "to paddle his own canoe."

These absurd promises inconsistent with the arguments of socialists themselves.

A socialist's attempt to defend these promises by reference to employees of the state post-office.

Equality of industrial opportunity for those who believe themselves possessed of exceptional talent and aspire "to rise."

Opportunities for such men involve costly experiment, and are necessarily limited.

Claimants who would waste them indefinitely more numerous than those who could use them profitably.

Such opportunities mean the granting to one man the control of other men by means of wage-capital.

Disastrous effects of granting such opportunities to all or even most of those who would believe themselves entitled to them.

True remedy for the difficulties besetting the problem of opportunity.

Ruskin on human demands. Needs and "romantic wishes." The former not largely alterable. The latter depend mainly on education.

The problem practically soluble by a wise moral education only, which will correlate demand and expectation with the personal capacities of the individual.

Relative equality of opportunity, not absolute equality, the true formula.

Equality of opportunity, though much talked about by socialists, is essentially a formula of competition, and opposed to the principles of socialism.

CHAPTER XVI

THE SOCIAL POLICY OF THE FUTURE

THE MORAL OF THIS BOOK

This book, though consisting of negative criticism and analysis of facts, and not trenching on the domain of practical policy and constructive suggestion, aims at facilitating a rational social policy by placing in their true perspective the main statical facts and dynamic forces of the modern economic world, which socialism merely confuses.

In pointing out the limitations of labour as a productive agency, and the dependence of the labourers on a class other than their own, it does not seek to represent the aspirations of the former to participate in the benefits of progress as illusory, but rather to place such aspirations on a scientific basis, and so to remove what is at present the principal obstacle that stands in the way of a rational and scientific social policy.

A CRITICAL EXAMINATION OF SOCIALISM

CHAPTER I

THE HISTORICAL BEGINNING OF SOCIALISM AS AN OSTENSIBLY SCIENTIFIC THEORY

Socialism, whatever may be its more exact definition, stands for an organisation of society, and more especially for an economic organisation, radically opposed to, and differing from, the organisation which prevails to-day. So much we may take for granted; but here, before going further, it is necessary to free ourselves from a very common confusion. When socialism, as thus defined, is spoken of as a thing that exists--as a thing that has risen and is spreading--two ideas are apt to suggest themselves to the minds of all parties equally, of which one coincides with facts, while the other does not, having, indeed, thus far at all events, no appreciable connection with them; and it is necessary to get rid of the false idea, and concern ourselves only with the true.

The best way in which I can make my meaning clear will be by referring to a point with regard to which the earlier socialistic thinkers may be fairly regarded as accurate and original critics. The so-called orthodox economists of the school of Mill and Ricardo accepted the capitalistic system as part of the order of nature, and their object was mainly to analyse the peculiar operations incident to it. The abler among the socialists were foremost in pointing out, on the contrary, a fact which now would not be denied by anybody: that capitalism in its present form is a comparatively modern phenomenon, owing its origin historically to the dissolution of the feudal system, and not having entered on its adolescence, or even on its independent childhood, till a time which may be roughly indicated as the middle of the eighteenth century. The immediate causes of its then accelerated development were, as the socialists insist, the rapid invention of new kinds of machinery, and more especially that of steam as a motor power, which together inaugurated a revolution in the methods of production generally. Production on a small scale gave way to production on a large. The independent weavers, for example, each with his own loom, were wholly unable to compete with the mechanisms of the new factory; their looms, by being superseded, were virtually taken away from them; and these men, formerly their own masters, working with their own implements, and living by the sale of their own individual products, were compelled to pass under the sway of a novel class, the capitalists; to work with implements owned by the capitalists, not themselves; and to live by the wages of their labour, not by their sale of the products of it.

Such, as the socialists insist, was the rise of the capitalistic system; and when once it had been adequately organised, as it first was, in England, it proceeded, they go on to observe, to spread itself with astonishing rapidity, all other methods disappearing before it, through their own comparative inefficiency. But when socialists or their opponents turn from capitalism to socialism, and speak of how socialism has risen and spread likewise, their language, as thus applied, has no meaning whatever unless it is interpreted in a totally new sense. For in the sense in which socialists speak of the rise and spread of capitalism, socialism has, up to the present time, if we except a number of small and unsuccessful experiments, never risen or spread or had any existence at all. Capitalism rose and spread as an actual working system, which multiplied and improved the material appliances of life in a manner beyond the reach of the older system displaced by it. It realised results of which previously mankind had hardly dreamed. Socialism, on the other hand, has risen and spread thus far, not as a system which is threatening to supersede capitalism by its actual success as an alternative system of production, but merely as a theory or belief that such an alternative is possible. Let us take any country or any city we please--for example, let us say Chicago, in which socialism is said to be achieving its most hopeful or most formidable triumphs--and we shall look in vain for a sign that the general productive process has been modified by socialistic principles in any particular whatsoever. Socialism has produced resolutions at endless public meetings; it has produced discontent and strikes; it has hampered production constantly. But socialism has never inaugurated an improved chemical process; it has never bridged an estuary or built an ocean liner; it has never produced or cheapened so much as a lamp or a frying-pan. It is a theory that such things could be accomplished by the practical application of its principles; but, except for the abortive experiments to which I have referred already, it is thus far a theory only, and it is as a theory only that we can examine it.

What, then, as a theory, are the distinctive features of socialism? Here is a question which, if we address it indiscriminately to all the types of people who now call themselves socialists, seems daily more impossible to answer; for every day the number of those is increasing who claim for their own opinions the title of socialistic, but whose quarrel with the existing system is very far from apparent, while less apparent still is the manner in which they propose to alter it. The persons to whom I refer consist mainly of academic students, professors, clergymen, and also of emotional ladies, who enjoy the attention of footmen in faultless liveries, and say their prayers out of prayer-books with jewelled clasps. All these persons unite in the general assertion that, whatever may be amiss with the world, the capitalistic system is responsible for it, and that somehow or other this system ought to be altered. But when we ask them to specify the details as to which alteration is necessary--what precisely are the parts of it which they wish to abolish and what, if these were abolished, they would introduce as a substitute--one of them says one thing, another of them says another, and nobody says anything on which three of them could act in concert.

Now, if socialism were confined to such persons as these, who are in America spoken of as the "parlour socialists," it would not only be impossible to tell what socialism actually was, but what it was or was not would be immaterial to any practical man. As a matter of fact, however, between socialism of this negligible kind--this sheet-lightning of sentiment reflected from a storm elsewhere--and the socialism which is really a factor to be reckoned with in the life of nations, we can start with drawing a line which, when once drawn, is unmistakable. Socialism being avowedly a theory which, in the first instance at all events, addresses itself to the many as distinct from and opposed to the few, it is only or mainly the fact of its adoption by the many which threatens to render it a practical force in politics. Its practical importance accordingly depends upon two things--firstly, on its possessing a form sufficiently definite to unite what would otherwise be a mass of heterogeneous units, by developing in all of them a common temper and purpose; and, secondly, on the number of those who can be taught to adopt and welcome it. The theory of socialism is, therefore, as a practical force, primarily that form of it which is operative among the mass of socialists; and when once we realise this, we shall have no further difficulty in discovering what the doctrines are with which, at all events, we must begin our examination. We are guided to our starting-point by the broad facts of history.

The rights of the many as opposed to the actual position of the few--a society in which all should be equal, not only in political status, but also in social circumstances; ideas such as these are as old as the days of Plato, and they have, from time to time in the ancient and the modern world, resulted in isolated and abortive attempts to realise them. In Europe such ideas were rife during the sixty or seventy years which followed the great political revolution in France. Schemes of society were formulated which were to carry this revolution further, and concentrate effort on industrial rather than political change. Pictures were presented to the imagination, and the world was invited to realise them, of societies in which all were workers on equal terms, and groups of fraternal citizens, separated no longer by the egoisms of the private home, dwelt together in palaces called "phalansteries," which appear to have been imaginary anticipations of the Waldorf-Astoria Hotel. Here lapped in luxury, they were to feast at common tables; and between meals the men were to work in the fields singing, while a lady accompanied their voices on a grand piano under a hedge. These pictures, however, agreeable as they were to the fancy, failed to produce any great effect on the multitudes; for the multitudes felt instinctively that they were too good to be true. That such was the case is admitted by socialistic historians themselves. Socialism during this period was, they say, in its "Utopian stage." It was not even sufficiently coherent to have acquired a distinctive name till the word "socialism" was coined in connection with the views of Owen, which suffered discredit from the failure of his attempts to put them into practice. Socialism in those days was a dream, but it was not science; and in a world which was rapidly coming to look upon science as supreme, nothing could convince men generally--not even the most ignorant--which had not, or was not supposed to have, the authority of science at the back of it.

Such being the situation, as the socialists accurately describe it, an eminent thinker arose who at last supplied what was wanting. He provided the unorganised aspirations, which by this time were known as socialism, with a formula which was at once definite, intelligible, and comprehensive, and had all the air of being rigidly scientific also. By this means thoughts and feelings, previously vague and fluid, like salts held in solution, were crystallised into a clear-cut theory which was absolutely the same for all; which all who accepted it could accept with the same intellectual confidence; and which thus became a moral and mental nucleus around which the efforts and hopes of a coherent party could group themselves.

Such was the feat accomplished by Karl Marx, through his celebrated treatise on Capital, which was published between fifty and sixty years ago, and which has, since then, throughout all Europe and America, been acclaimed as the Magna Charta, or the Bible, of "scientific socialism."

Whatever may be the change which, as a theory, socialism has subsequently undergone--and changes there have been which will presently occupy our attention--it is with the theory of Marx, and the temper of mind resulting from it, that socialism, regarded as a practical force, begins; and among the majority of socialists this theory is predominant still. In view, therefore, of the requirements of logic, of history, and of contemporary facts, our own examination must begin with the theory of Marx likewise.

CHAPTER II

THE THEORY OF MARX AND THE EARLIER SOCIALISTS SUMMARISED

All radical revolutions which are advocated in the interests of the people are commended to the people, and the people are invited to accomplish them, on the ground that majorities are, if they would only realise it, capable of moulding society in any manner they please. As applied to matters of legislation and government, this theory is sufficiently familiar to everybody. It has been elaborated in endless detail, and has expressed itself in the constitutions of all modern democracies. What Karl Marx did, and did for the first time, was to invest this theory of the all-efficiency of the majority with a definiteness, in respect of distribution of wealth, similar to that with which it had been invested already in respect of the making of laws and the dictation of national policies.

The practical outcome of the scientific reasoning of Marx is summed up in the formula which has figured as the premise and conclusion of every congress of his followers, of every book or manifesto published by them, and of every propagandist oration uttered by them at street-corners, namely, "All wealth is produced by labour, therefore to the labourers all wealth is due"--a doctrine in itself not novel if taken as a pious generality, but presented by Marx as the outcome of an elaborate system of economics.

The efficiency of this doctrine as an instrument of agitation is obvious. It appeals at once to two universal instincts: the instinct of cupidity and the instinct of universal justice. It stimulates the labourers to demand more than they receive already, and it stimulates to demand the more on the ground that they themselves have produced it. It teaches them that the wealth of every man who is not a manual labourer is something stolen from themselves which ought to be and which can be restored to them.

Now, whatever may be the value of such teaching as a contribution to economic science, it illustrates by its success one cardinal truth, and by implication it bears witness to another. The first truth is that, no matter how desirable any object may be which is obtruded on the imagination of anybody, nobody will bestir himself in a practical way to demand it until he can be persuaded to believe that its attainment is practically possible. The other is this: that the possibilities of redistributing wealth depend on the causes by which wealth is produced. All wealth, says Marx, can practically be appropriated by the labourers. But why? Because the labourers themselves comprise in their own labour all the forces that produce it. If its production necessitated the activity of any persons other than themselves, these other persons would inevitably have some control over its distribution; since if it were distributed in a manner of which these other persons disapproved, it would be open to them to refuse to take part in its production any longer; and there would, in consequence, be no wealth, or less wealth, to distribute.

Let us, then, examine the precise sense and manner in which this theory of labour as the sole producer of wealth is elaborated and defended by Marx in his Bible of Scientific Socialism. His argument, though the expression of it is very often pedantic and encumbered with superfluous mathematical formul? is ingenious and interesting, and is associated with historical criticism which, in spite of its defects, is valuable. Marx was, indeed, foremost among those thinkers already referred to who first insisted on the fact that the economic conditions of to-day are mainly a novel development of others which went before them, and that, having their roots in history, they must be studied by the historical method. He recognised, however, that for practical purposes each age must concern itself with its own environment; and his logical starting-point is an analysis of wealth-production as it exists to-day. He begins by insisting on the fact that labour in the modern world is divided with such a general and such an increasing minuteness that each labour produces one kind of product only, of which he himself can consume but a small fraction, and often consumes nothing. His own product, therefore, has for him the character of wealth only because he is able to exchange it for commodities of other kinds; and the amount of wealth represented by it depends upon what the quantity of other assorted commodities, which he can get in exchange for it, is. What, then, is the common measure, in accordance with which, as a fact, one kind of commodity will exchange for any other, or any others? For his answer to this question Marx goes to the orthodox economists of his time--the recognised exponents of the system against which his own arguments were directed--and notably, among these, to Ricardo; and, adopting Ricardo's conclusions, as though they were axiomatic, he asserts that the measure of exchange between one class of commodities and another--such, for example, as cigars, printed books, and chronometers--is the amount of manual labour, estimated in terms of time, which is on an average necessary to the production of each of them. His meaning in this respect is illustrated with pictorial vividness by his teaching with regard to the form in which the measure of exchange should embody itself. This, he said, ought not to be gold or silver, but "labour-certificates," which would indicate that whoever possessed them had laboured for so many hours in producing no matter what, and which would purchase anything else, or any quantity of anything else, representing an equal expenditure of labour of any other kind.

Having thus settled, as it seemed to him beyond dispute, that manual labour, estimated in terms of time, is the sole source and measure of economic values or of wealth, Marx goes on to point out that, by the improvement of industrial methods, labour in the modern world has been growing more and more productive, so that each labour-hour results in an increased yield of commodities. Thus a man who a couple of centuries ago could have only just kept himself alive by the products of his entire labour-day, can now keep himself alive by the products of half or a quarter of it. The products of the remainder of his labour-day are what Marx called a "surplus value," meaning by this phrase all that output of wealth which is beyond what is practically necessary to keep the labourer alive. But what, he asks, becomes of this surplus? Does it go to the labourers who have produced it? No, he replies. On the contrary, as fast as it is produced, it is abstracted from the labourer in a manner, which he goes on to analyse, by the capitalist.

Marx here advances to the second stage of his argument. Capital, as he conceives of it, is the tools or instruments of production; and modern capital for him means those vast aggregates of machinery by the use of which in most industries the earlier implements have been displaced. Now, here, says Marx, the capitalist is sure to interpose with the objection that the increased output of wealth is due, not to labour, but to the machinery, and that the labourer, as such, has consequently no claim on it. But to this objection Marx is ready with the following answer--that the machinery itself is nothing but past labour in disguise. It is past labour crystallised, or embodied in an external form, and used by present labour to assist itself in its own operations. Every wheel, crank, and connecting-rod, every rivet in every boiler, owes its shape and its place to labour, and labour only. Labour, therefore--the labour of the average multitude--remains the sole agent in the production of wealth, after all.

Capital, however, as thus understood, has, he says, this peculiarity--that, being labour in an externalised and also in a permanent form, it is capable of being detached from the labourers and appropriated by other people; and the essence of modern capitalism is neither more nor less than this--the appropriation of the instruments of production by a minority who are not producers. So long as the implements of production were small and simple, and such that each could be used by one man or family, the divorce between the labourer and his implements was not easy to accomplish; but in proportion as these simple implements were developed into the aggregated mechanisms of the factory, each of which aggregates was used in common by hundreds and even by thousands of labourers, the link between the implement and the user was broken by an automatic process; for a single organised mechanism used by a thousand men could not, in the nature of things, be owned by each one of the thousand individually, and collective ownership by all of them was an idea as yet unborn. Under these circumstances, with the growth of modern machinery, the ownership of the implements of production passed, by what Marx looked upon as a kind of historical fatality, into the hands of a class whose activities were purely acquisitive, and had no true connection with the process of production at all; and this class, he said, constitutes the capitalists of the modern world.

The results of this process have, according to him, been as follows: Society has become divided into two contrasted groups--an enormous group, and a small one. The enormous group--the great body of every nation--the people--

the labouring mass--the one true producing power--has been left without any implements by means of which its labour can exert itself, and these implements have been monopolised by the small group alone. The people at large, in fact, have become like the employees of a single mill-owner, who have no choice but to work within the walls of that mill or starve; and the possessing class at large has become like the owner of such a single mill, who, holding the keys of life and death in his hands, is able to impose on the mill-workers almost any terms he pleases as the price of admission to his premises and to the privilege of using his machinery; and the price which such an owner, so situated, will exact (such was the contention of Marx) inevitably must come, and historically has come, to this--namely, the entire amount of goods which the labouring class produces, except such a minimum as will just enable its members to keep themselves in working order, and to reproduce their kind. Thus all capital, as at present owned, all profits, and all interest on capital, are neither more nor less than thefts from the labouring class of commodities which are produced by the labouring class alone.

The argument of Marx is not, however, finished yet. There remains a third part of it which we still have to consider. Writing as he did, almost half a century ago, he said that the process of capitalistic appropriation had not--yet completed itself. A remnant of producers on a restricted scale survived, still forming a middle class, which was neither rich nor poor. But, he continued, in all capitalistic countries, a new movement, inevitable from the first, had set in, and its pace was daily accelerating. Just as the earlier capitalists swallowed up most of the small producers, so were the great capitalists swallowing up the smaller, and the middle class which survived was disappearing day by day. Wages, meanwhile, were regulated by an iron law. Under the system of capitalism it was an absolute impossibility that they could rise. As he put it, in language which has since become proverbial, "The rich are getting richer, the poor poorer, the middle class is being crushed out," and the time, he continued, was in sight already--it would arrive, according to him, before the end of the nineteenth century--when nothing would be left but a handful of idle and preposterous millionaires on the one hand, and a mass of miserable ragamuffins who provided all the millions on the other, having for themselves only enough food and clothing to enable them to move their muscles and protect their nakedness from the frost. Then, said Marx, when this contrast has completed itself, the situation will be no longer tolerable. "Then the knell of the capitalistic system will have sounded." The producers will assert themselves under the pressure of an irresistible impulse; they will repossess themselves of the implements of production of which they have been so long deprived. "The expropriators will in their turn be expropriated," and the labourers thenceforth owning the implements of production collectively, all the wealth of the world will forever afterwards be theirs.

This concluding portion of the gospel of Marx--its prophecies--has been in many of its details so completely falsified by events that even his most ardent disciples no longer insist on it. I have only mentioned it here because of the further light which it throws on what alone, in this discussion, concerns us-- namely, the Marxian theory of labour as the sole producer of wealth, and the absolute nullity, so far as production goes, of every form of activity associated with the possession of capital, or with any class but the labouring.

This theory of production, then, which has been the foundation of socialism as a party and which is still its foundation for the great majority of socialists, we will now examine in detail, and, considering how complex are the processes of production in the modern world, ask how far it gives us, or fails to give us, even an approximately complete account of them.

We shall find that, in spite of the plausibility with which the talent of Marx invested it, this basic doctrine of so-called scientific socialism is the greatest intellectual mare's-nest of the century which has just ended; and when once we have realised with precision on what, in the modern world, the actual efficiency of the productive process depends, we shall see that the analysis of Marx bears about the same relation to the economic facts of to-day that the child's analysis of matter into the four traditional elements, or the doctrine of Thales that everything is made of water, bears to the facts of chemistry as modern science has revealed them to us.

CHAPTER III

THE ROOT ERROR OF THE MARXIAN THEORY. ITS OMISSION OF DIRECTIVE ABILITY. ABILITY AND LABOUR DEFINED

In approaching the opinions of another, from whom we are about to differ, we gain much in clearness if at starting we can find some point of agreement with him. In the case of Marx we can find this without difficulty, for the first observation which our subject will naturally suggest to us is an admission that, within limits, his theory of production is true. Whatever may be the agencies which are required to produce wealth, human effort is one of them; and into whatever kinds this necessary agency may divide itself, one kind must always be labour, in the sense in which Marx understood it--in other words, that use of the hands and muscles by which the majority of mankind have always gained their livelihood.

It is, moreover, easy to point out actual cases in which all the wealth that is produced is produced by labour only. The simplest of such cases are supplied us by the lowest savages, who manage, by their utmost exertions, to provide themselves with the barest necessaries. Such cases show that labour, wherever it exists, produces at least a minimum of what men require; for if it were not so there would be no men to labour. Such cases show also another thing. The most primitive races possess rude implements of some kind, which any pair of hands can fashion, just as any pair of hands can use them. These rude implements are capital in its embryonic form; and so far as they go, they verify the Marxian theory that capital is nothing but past labour crystallised.

But we need not, in order to see labour, past and present, operating and producing in a practically unalloyed condition, go to savage or even semi-civilised countries. The same thing may be seen among groups of peasant proprietors, which still survive here and there in the remoter parts of Europe. These men and their families, by their own unaided labour, produce nearly everything which they eat and wear and use. Mill, in his treatise on Political Economy, gives us an account of this condition of things, as prevailing among the peasants in certain districts of Germany. "They labour early and late," he says, quoting from a German eulogist. "They plod on from day to day and from year to year, the most untirable of human animals." The German writer admires them as men who are their own masters. Mill holds them up as a shining and instructive example of the magic effect of ownership in intensifying human labour. In any case such men are examples of two things-- of labour operating as the sole productive agency, and also of such labour self-intensified to its utmost pitch. And what does the labour of these men produce? According to the authority from which Mill quotes, it produces just enough to keep them above the level of actual want. Here, then, we have an unexceptionable example of the wealth-producing power of labour pure and simple; and if we imagine an entire nation of men who, as their own masters, worked under liked conditions, we should have an example of the same thing on a larger and more instructive scale. We should have a whole nation which produced only just enough to keep it above the level of actual bodily want.

And now let us turn from production in an imaginary nation such as this, and compare it with production at large among the civilised nations of to-day. Nobody could insist on the contrast between the efficiency of the two processes more strongly than do the socialists themselves. The aggregate wealth of the civilised nations to-day is, they say, so enormous--it consists of such a multitude of daily renewed goods and services--that luxuries undreamed of by the labourer of earlier times might easily be made as abundant for every household as water. In other words, if we take a million men, admittedly consisting of labourers pure and simple in the first place, and the same number of men exerting themselves under modern conditions in the second place, the industrial efforts of the second million are, hour for hour, infinitely more productive than the industrial efforts of the first. If, for example, we take the case of England, and compare the product produced per head of the industrial population towards the close of the seventeenth century, with the product produced less than two centuries afterwards, at the time when Marx was writing his work on Capital, the later product will, according to the estimate of statisticians, stand to the earlier in the proportion of thirty-three to seven.

Now, if we adopt the scientific theory of Marx that labour pure and simple is the sole producer of wealth, and that labour is productive in proportion to the hours devoted to it, how has it happened--this is our crucial question-- that the amount of labour which produced seven at one period should produce thirty-three at another? How are we to explain the presence of the additional twenty-six?

The answer of Marx, and of those who reason like him, is that, owing to the development of knowledge, mechanical and chemical especially, and the consequent development of industrial methods and machinery, labour as a whole has itself become more productive. But to say this is merely begging the question. To what is this development of knowledge, of methods, and of machinery due? Is it due to such labour as that of the "untirable human animals," to which Mill refers as an example of labour in its intensest form? In a word, does ordinary labour, or the industrial effort of the majority, contain in itself any principle of advance at all?

We must, in order to do justice to any theory, consider not only the points on which its exponents lay the greatest stress, but also those which they recognise as implied in it, or which we may see to be implied in it ourselves. And if we consider the theory of Marx in this way, we shall see that labour, in the sense in which he understands the word, does contain principles of advance which are of two distinguishable kinds.

One of these is recognised by Marx himself. Just as, when he says that labour is the sole productive agency, he assumes the gifts of nature, which provide it with something to work upon, so, when he conceives of labour as the effort of hand and muscle, he assumes a human mind behind these by which hand and muscle are directed. Such being the case, he expressly admits also that mind is in some cases a more efficient director than in others, and is able to train the hands and muscles of the labourer, so that these acquire the quality which is commonly called skill. Ruskin, who asserted, like Marx, that labour is the sole producer, used in this respect a precisely similar argument. He defined skill as faculty which exceptional powers of mind impart to the hands of those by whom such powers are possessed, from the bricklayer who, in virtue of mere alertness and patience, can lay in an hour more bricks than his fellows, up to a Raphael, whose hands can paint a Madonna, while another man's could hardly be trusted to distemper a wall evenly.

Now, in skill, as thus defined, we have doubtless a correct explanation of how mere labour--the manual effort of the individual--may produce, in the case of some men, goods whose value is great, and goods, in the case of other men, whose value is comparatively small; and since some epochs are more fertile in developed skill than others, an equal amount of labour on the part of the same community may produce, in one century, goods of greater aggregate value than it was able to produce in the century that went before it. But these goods, whose superior value is due to exceptional skill--or, as would commonly be said, to qualities of superior craftsmanship--though they form some of the most coveted articles of the wealth of the modern world, are not typical of it; and from the point of view of the majority, they are the part of it which is least important. The goods whose value is due to exceptional craftsmanship--such as an illuminated manuscript, for example, or a vase by Benvenuto Cellini--are always few in number, and can be possessed by the few only. The distinctive feature of wealth-production in the modern world, on the contrary, is the multiplication of goods relatively to the number of the producers of them, and the consequent cheapening of each article individually. The skill of the craftsman gives an exceptional value to the particular articles on which his own hands are engaged. It does not communicate itself to the labour of the ordinary men around him. The agency which causes the increasing and sustains the increased output of necessaries, comforts, and conveniences in the progressive nations of to-day must necessarily be an agency of some kind or other which raises the productivity of industrial exertion as a whole. Those, therefore, who, in spite of the fact that the productivity of modern communities has, relatively to their numbers, undergone an increase which is general, still maintain that the sole productive agency is labour, must seek for an explanation of this increase in some other fact than skill.

And without transgressing the limits which the theory of Marx imposes on us, such a further fact is very easy to find. Adam Smith opens his Wealth of Nations with a discussion of it. The chief cause, he says, which in all progressive countries increases the productive power of the individual labourer, is not the development among a few of potentialities which are above the average, but a more effective development of potentialities common to all, in consequence of labour being divided, so that each man devotes his life to the doing of some one thing. Thus if ten ordinary men were to engage in the business of pin-making, each making every part of every pin for himself, each man would probably complete but one pin in a day. But if each man makes one part, and nothing else but that, thus repeating incessantly a single series of motions, each will acquire the knack of working with such rapidity that the ten together will make daily, not ten pins, but some thousands. Here we have labour divided by its different applications, but not requiring different degrees of capacity. We have the average labour of the average man still. And here we have a fact which, unlike the fact of skill--a thing in its nature confined to the few only--affords a real explanation, up to a certain point, of how ordinary labour as a whole, without ceasing to be ordinary labour, may rise from a lower to a higher grade of efficiency.

But such simple divisions of labour as those which are here in question fail, for a reason which will be specified in another moment, to carry us far in the history of industrial progress. They do but bring us to the starting-point of production as it exists to-day. The efficiency of productive effort has made all its most astounding advances since the precise time at which the Wealth of Nations was written; and these advances we shall find that it is quite impossible to explain merely by a further division of average and equal labour. Such a further division has no doubt been an element of the process; but it is an explanation which itself requires explaining. Even in Adam Smith's time two other factors were at work, which have ever since been growing in magnitude and importance; and the secret of modern production lies, we shall find, in these. I call them two, but fundamentally there is only one, for that which is most obvious, and of which I shall speak first, is explainable only as the direct result of the second. This, the most obvious factor, is the modern development of machinery. The other is the growing application of exceptional mental powers, not to the manual labour of the men by whom these powers are possessed, but to the _process of directing and co-ordinating the divided labours of others_.

Now, as to machinery, Marx and his followers, as we have seen, maintain that it represents nothing but the average labour of the past; and so long as it exists only in its smaller and simpler forms, the devising and constructing of which are not referable to any faculties which we are able to distinguish from those of the average labourer, we have further seen that the theory of Marx holds good. Labour produces alike both the finished goods and its implements. But in proportion as machines or other contrivances, such as vessels, grow in size or complexity, and embody, as they do in their more modern developments, ingenuity of the highest and knowledge of the most abstruse kinds, the situation changes; and we are able to identify certain faculties as essential to the ultimate result, which affect the work of the labourers, but which do not emanate from themselves. Any three men of average strength and intelligence might make a potter's wheel together, or build a small boat together, as they frequently do now, their several tasks being interchangeable, or assigned to each of them by easy mutual agreement. The business of directing labour has not separated itself from the actual business of labouring. Each man knows the object of what he does, and can co-ordinate that object with the object of what is done by his fellows. But when the ultimate result is something so vast and complicated that a thousand men instead of three have to co-operate in the production of it, when a million pieces of metal, some large and some minute, have to be cast, filed, turned, rolled, or bent, so that finally they may all coalesce into a single mechanical organism, no one labourer sees further than the task which he performs himself. He cannot adjust his work to that of another man, who is probably working a quarter of a mile away from him, and he has in most cases no idea whatever of how the two pieces of work are related to each other. Each labourer has simply to perform his work in accordance with directions which emanate from some mind other than his own, and the whole practical value of what the labourers do depends on the quality of the directions which are thus given to each.

In other words, in proportion as the industrial process is enhanced in productivity by the concentration on it of the higher faculties of mankind, there is an increasing fission of this process as a whole into two kinds of activity represented by two different groups. We have no longer _merely_-- although we have this _still_--an increasing division of labour; but we have the labourers of all kinds and grades separating themselves into one group on the one hand, and the men who direct their labour, as a separate group, on the other hand.

The function of the directive faculties, as applied thus to the operations of modern labour, can perhaps be most easily illustrated by the case of a printed book. Let us take two editions of ten thousand copies each, similarly printed, and priced at six shillings a copy; the one being an edition of a book so dull that but twenty copies can be sold of it, the other of a book so interesting that the public buys the whole ten thousand. Now, apart from its negligible value as so many tons of waste paper, each pile of books represents economic wealth only in proportion to the quantity of it for which the vendors can find purchasers. Hence we have in the present case two piles of printed paper which, regarded as paper patterned with printer's ink, are similar, but one of which is wealth to the extent of three thousand pounds, while the other is wealth to the extent of no more than six pounds. And to what is the difference between these two values due? It obviously cannot be due to the manual labour of the compositors, for this, both in kind and quantity, is in each case the same. It is due to the special directions under which the labour of the compositors is performed. But these directions do not emanate from the men by whose hands the types are arranged in a given order.

They come from the author, who conveys them to the compositors through his manuscript; which manuscript, considered under its economic aspect, is neither more nor less than a series of minute orders, which modify from second to second every movement of the compositors' hands, and determine the subsequent results of every impress of the type on paper; one mind thus, by directing the labour of others, imparting the quality of much wealth or of little or of none, to every one of the ten thousand copies of which the edition is composed.

Similarly when a man invents, and brings into practical use, some new and successful apparatus such, let us say, as the telephone, the same situation repeats itself. The new apparatus is an addition to the world's wealth, not because so many scraps of wood, brass, nickel, vulcanite, and such and such lengths of wire are shaped, stretched, and connected with sufficient manual dexterity--for the highest dexterity is very often employed in the making of contrivances which turn out to be futile--but because each of its parts is fashioned in obedience to certain designs with which this dexterity, as such, has nothing at all to do. The apparatus is successful, and an addition to the world's wealth, because the designs of the inventor, just like the author's manuscript, constitute a multitude of injunctions proceeding from a master-mind, which is not the mind of those by whose hands they are carried into execution.

And with the direction of labour generally, whether in the production of machinery or the use of the machinery in the production of goods for the public, the case is again the same. We have manual labour of a given kind and quality, which assists in producing what is wanted or not wanted--what is so much wealth or simply so much refuse, in accordance with the manner in which all this labour is directed by faculties specifically different from those exercised by the manual labourers themselves.

And now we are in a position to sum up in a brief and decisive formula what the difference between the sets of faculties thus contrasted is. It is not essentially a difference between lower and higher, for some forms of labour, such as that of the great painter, may be morally higher than some forms of direction. The difference is one not of degree, but of kind, and includes two different psycho-physical processes. Labour, from the most ordinary up to the rarest kind, _is the mind or the brain of one man affecting that man's own hands_, and the single task on which his hands happen to be engaged. The directive faculties are the mind or the brain of one man simultaneously affecting the hands of any number of other men, and through their hands the simultaneous tasks of all of them, no matter how various these tasks may be.

CHAPTER IV

THE ERRORS OF MARX, CONTINUED. CAPITAL AS THE IMPLEMENT OF ABILITY

The human activities and faculties, then, which are involved in the production of modern wealth, are not, as Marx says--and as the orthodox economists said, whom he rightly calls his masters, and as their followers still say--of one kind--namely, those embodied in the individual task-work of the individual, to which Marx, Ricardo, and Mill alike give the name of "labour"; they are of two kinds. And this, indeed, the earlier economists recognised, as we may see by Mill's casual admission that the progress of industrial effort depends before all things on thought and the advance of knowledge. But they recognised the fact in a general way only. How thought and knowledge affected the industrial process they made no attempt to explain, otherwise than by comprehending them on occasion under the common name of labour, which they assigned throughout most of their arguments to manual task-work only.

Now, it is doubtless true that, as a mere matter of verbal propriety, this general sense may be given to the word "labour," if we please; but if in discussing the efforts which produce wealth we admit that these efforts are not of one kind but two, and if the word "labour" is, in nine cases out of ten, employed with the definite intention of designating only one of them, it is impossible to reason about the industrial process intelligibly, so long as we apply also the same name to the other. We might as well use the word "man"--as with reference to some problems we are perfectly right in doing--to designate both men and women, and then attempt to discuss the relations between the two sexes.

For the directive faculties, so essentially distinct from those to which universal custom has allocated the name of labour, it is difficult to find a name equally convenient and satisfying. In default of a better, I have, on former occasions, applied to it the name of Ability; and this will serve our purpose here--especially as it is a name which has been, of recent years, applied by many of the more thoughtful socialists themselves to certain activities of a mental and moral kind, which their conception of labour cannot be made to include, but which they are beginning to recognise as playing some part in production. We must remember, however, that we are using it in a strictly technical sense, which will in some respects be narrower than the ordinary, and in some more comprehensive. It will exclude all kinds of cleverness unapplied to economic production; and will include many powers, in so far as such production is affected by them, to the expression of whose scope and character it may sometimes appear inadequate.[1]

And now when we have come thus far, a quite new question arises. We have seen how ability is, by its direction of labour, the chief agency in that process which produces wealth to-day, and how it makes the amount produced, relatively to the number of the producers, so incomparably greater than it ever was under any previous system. We have now to consider the means by which this faculty of direction is exercised.

In order to understand this, we must turn our attention again to capital, as something distinct and detached from the human efforts that have produced it; and we shall find that the conception of it which dominated the thought of Marx, and that which dominates the thought of the orthodox school of economists, either excludes altogether, or fails to reveal the nature of, that particular force and function of it which, in the modern world, are fundamental.

Capital is divided traditionally into two kinds, technically called "fixed" and "circulating." By fixed capital, which is what Marx had mainly in view, is meant machinery, and the works and structures connected with it; and it is called "fixed" on account of its comparative permanence. By circulating capital is meant, as Adam Smith puts it, any stock of those consumable commodities which, produced by the aid of machinery, the merchant or the store-keeper buys in order to sell them at a profit; and it is called "circulating" because the commodities which are sold to-day are replaced by new ones of an equivalent kind to-morrow.

Now, as to fixed capital, or the endlessly elaborated machinery of the modern world, we have seen already that this is, in its distinctive features, not, as Marx declared it to be, a crystallisation of labour, but a crystallisation of the ability by which labour has been directed; but this revised explanation tells us nothing of the means by which the direction is accomplished. Still less is any light thrown on the question by the nature of circulating capital, as Adam Smith understands it.

The kind of capital which alone concerns us here is a kind which resembles circulating capital in respect of its material form, and is often indeed in this respect identical with it; but it differs from circulating capital in respect of the use made of it. Such capital we may call wage-capital. Wage-capital, although in practice it disguises itself under the form of money, is essentially a stock of goods which are the daily necessaries of life, but which, instead of being sold to the public, like the goods of the store-keeper, at a profit, are distributed by their possessor among a special group of labourers on conditions. The first of these is naturally that the labourers do work of some sort. The second condition, and the one that concerns us here, is that, besides doing work of some sort, each labourer shall do the work which the distributer of the goods prescribes to him.

Here we have before us the means by which, in the modern world, the ability of the few directs the labour of the many; and, in proportion to the quality and intensity of the directive powers that are exercised, adds to the value of the results which this labour would have produced otherwise. Thus in wage-capital we have the capital of the modern world in what dynamically is its primary and parent form--a kind of capital which improved machinery is always tending to augment, but of whose use the machinery itself, its renewal, and its continued improvement, are the consequences.

That such is the case might be illustrated by any number of familiar examples. A man invents a new machine having some useful purpose--let us say the production of some new kind of manure, which will double the fertility of every field in the country. In order to put this machine on the market, and make it a fact instead of a mere conception, the first thing necessary is, as every human being knows, that the inventor shall possess, or acquire, the control of capital. And what is the next step? When the capital is provided, how will it first be used? It will be used in the form of wages, or articles of daily consumption, which will be distributed among a certain number of mechanics and other labourers, on condition that they set about fashioning, in certain prescribed groups, so much metal into so many prescribed shapes--some of them shaping it into wheels, some into knives and rollers, some into sieves, rods, cranks, cams, and eccentrics, in accordance with patterns which have never been followed previously; and of all these individual operations the new machine, as a practical implement, is the result. The machine is new, and it is an addition to the wealth-producing powers of the world, not because it embodies so much labour, but because it embodies so much labour directed in a new way; and it is only by means of the conditions which the possession of wage-capital enables the inventor or his partners to impose upon every one of the labourers that the machine, as a practical implement, comes into existence at all.

Hence we see that Marx was at once right and wrong when he said that modern capitalism is, in its essence, monopoly. It is monopoly; but it is not primarily, as Marx thought, a passive monopoly of improved instruments of production. It is primarily a monopoly of products which are essential to the life of the labourer; and it is a monopoly of these, not in the invidious sense that the monopolists retain them for their own personal consumption, as they do in the case of rare wines and fabrics, which can, from the nature of the case, be enjoyed by a few only. It is a monopoly of them in the sense that the monopolists have such a control over their distribution as enables them to control the purely technical actions of those persons who ultimately own and consume the whole of them.[2]

Modern capital, then, I repeat, is primarily wage-capital, such capital as modern machinery being the direct result of its application; and wage-capital is productive, not in virtue of any quality inherent in itself, but merely because as a fact, under the modern system, it constitutes the reins by which the exceptional ability of a few guides the labour, skilled or unskilled, of the many. It is the means by which the commonest labourer, who hardly knows the rule of three, is made to work as though he were master of the abstruest branches of mathematics; by which the artisan who only has a smattering--if he has as much as that--of mechanics, metallurgy, chemistry, is made to work as though all the sciences had been assimilated by his single brain.

Let any one consider, for example, one of the great steel bridges which now throw their single spans over waters such as the Firth of Forth. These structures are crystallised labour, doubtless, but they are, in their distinctive features, not crystallised labour as such. They are crystallised mechanics, crystallised chemistry, crystallised mathematics--in short, crystallised intellect, knowledge, imagination, and executive capacity, of kinds which hardly exist in a dozen minds out of a million; and labour conduces to the production of such astonishing structures only because it submits itself to the guidance of these intellectual leaders. And the same is the case with modern production generally. Though labour is essential to the production of wealth even in the smallest quantities, the distinguishing productivity of industry in the modern world depends not on the labour, but on the ability with which the labour is directed; and in the modern world the primary function of capital is that of providing ability with its necessary instrument of direction.

No unprejudiced person, who is capable of coherent thought, can, when the matter is thus plainly stated, possibly deny this. That it cannot be denied will be shown in the two following chapters by recent admissions on the part of socialists themselves, the more thoughtful of whom have now virtually abandoned the earlier theoretical framework of socialism altogether, and are trying to substitute a new one, with which we will deal later, and which will indeed prove the main subject of our inquiry.

FOOTNOTES:

[1] When I insisted on this distinction between "labour" and "ability" in America, innumerable critics met me with two objections. One of these, as stated by a writer who confessed himself otherwise in entire agreement with me, was this: "It is impossible, as Mr. Mallock attempts to do, to draw a hard-and-fast line between mental effort and muscular." No such attempt is made. As I pointed out in one of my speeches, many kinds of "labour" (_e.g._ that of the great painter) exhibit higher mentality than do many kinds of ability. Further, I pointed out that, in a technical sense, the same effort may be either an effort of labour or ability, according to its application. Thus, if a singer sings to an audience, his effort is technically "labour," because it ends with the single task; but if he sings so as to produce a gramophone record, his effort is an act of "ability," for he influences the products of other men, by whom the records are multiplied. The second objection was expressed by one of my critics thus: "I say that all productive effort is labour.... I dare you to tell any one of these genii that they are not labourers." Another critic said: "Just as 'land' in economics means all the forces of nature, so does 'labour' mean

all the forces of man. Why, then, speak of ability?" These criticisms are purely verbal. If we like to take "labour" as a collective name for all forms of human effort, we can of course do so; but in that case we must find other differential names for the different forces of effort individually. To give them all the same name is not to explain them. It is to tie them all up in a parcel.

[2] If this fact requires any further exemplification, we can find one on a large scale in the pages of Marx himself. According to him the first appreciable capitalistic movement--the first leaping of the modern system in the womb--took place in the English cloth trade about four hundred years ago. Now, if capitalism were merely, as according to Marx it is, a passive monopoly by some men of implements which have been produced by others, the pioneers of capitalism in the reign of Henry VIII. would have got into their possession all the hand-looms then in use; they would have taken their toll in kind from all whom they allowed to use them; and there the matter would have ended. The looms of to-day would be the looms of four hundred years ago. The passive ownership of machines does nothing to improve their construction. If a gang of ignorant thieves could steal all the watches in America, and then let them out to the public at so much a month or year, this would not convert the three-dollar watches into chronometers. And how little mere labour, or the experience gained by labour, tends to improve the implements which the labourer uses is shown by the fact that the looms which wove Anne Boleyn's petticoats were practically the same as the looms which wove those of Semiramis.

CHAPTER V

REPUDIATION OF MARX BY MODERN SOCIALISTS. THEIR RECOGNITION OF DIRECTIVE ABILITY

In saying that, up to the point which our argument has thus far reached, the more thoughtful among the socialists to-day concede and even assert its truth, I have evidence in view of a very opposite kind. When I delivered, as I did recently, a series of addresses on socialism to various meetings in America, I approached the subject in the manner in which I have approached it here. I began with the process of production pure and simple, and I showed how crude and childish, as applied to production in modern times, was the analysis of Marx and all the earlier socialists. I showed, as I have shown here, that, the amount of labour being given, the quantity and quality of wealth that will result from its exercise depend on the ability with which by means of wage-capital this labour is directed.

The two addresses in which these points were elaborated had no sooner been delivered than, from all parts of the country, through newspapers and private letters, and sometimes by word of mouth, socialists of various types addressed themselves to the business of replying to me. These replies, whatever may have been their differences otherwise, all took the form of a declaration that I was only wasting my time in exposing the doctrine that labour is the sole producer of wealth, and in laying such stress on the part played by directive ability; for no serious socialist of the present day any longer believed the one, or failed to recognise the other. Thus one of my critics told me that what I ought to do was "to discuss the principles of socialism as understood and accepted by the intelligent disciples, and not the worn-out and discredited theories of Marx." Another was good enough to tell me that I had "cleverly accomplished the task of exposing the errors of Marx, both of premise and of logic"; but the leaders of socialistic thought "in its later developments" had, he proceeded to say, long ago outgrown these. A third wrote me a letter bristling with all kinds of challenges, and asked me if I thought, for example, that socialists were such fools as not to recognise that the talents of an inventor like Mr. Edison increased the productivity of labour by the new direction which they gave to it. I might multiply similar quotations, but one more will be enough here. It is taken from a long article directed against myself by Mr. Hillquit--a writer to whom my special attention was called as by far the most accomplished exponent, among the militant socialists of America, of socialism in its most logical and most highly developed form. "It requires," said Mr. Hillquit, "no special genius to demonstrate that all labour is not alike, nor equally productive. It is still more obvious that common manual labour is impotent to produce the wealth of modern nations--that organisation, direction, and control are essential to productive work in the field of modern production, and are just as much a factor in it as mere physical effort."[3]

But we need not confine ourselves to my own late critics in America. The general history of socialism as a reasoned theory is practically the same in one country as in another. The intellectual socialists in England, among whom Mr. Bernard Shaw and Mr. Sidney Webb are prominent, express themselves in even plainer terms with regard to the part which directive ability, as opposed to labour, plays in the modern world. "Ability," says Mr. Shaw, employing the very word, is often the factor which determines whether a given industry shall make a loss of five per cent. or else a profit of twenty; and Mr. Webb, as we shall have occasion to see presently, carries the argument further, and states it in greater detail.

Why, then, it may be asked, should a critic of contemporary socialism think it worth while to expose with so much minuteness a fallacy which intellectual socialists now all agree in repudiating, and to insist with such emphasis on facts which they profess to recognise as self-evident? To this question there are two answers.

One of these I indicated at the close of our opening chapter; and this at the cost of what in logic is a mere digression, it will be desirable, for practical purposes, to state it with greater fulness.

Admissions and assertions, such as those which I have just now quoted, do, no doubt, represent a definite intellectual advance which has taken place in the theory of socialism, among those who are its most thoughtful exponents, and in a certain sense its leaders. They represent what these leaders think and say among themselves, and what they put forward when disputing with opponents who are competent to criticise them. But what they do not represent is socialism as still preached to the populace, or the doctrine which is still vital for socialists as a popular party. This is still, just as it was originally, the socialism of Marx in an absolutely unamended form. It is the doctrine that the manual efforts of the vast multitude of labourers, directed only by the minds of the individual labourers themselves, produce all the wealth of the world; that the holding of any of this wealth by any other class whatever stands for nothing but a system of legalised plunder; and that the labourers need only inaugurate a legislation of a new kind in order to secure and enjoy what always was by rights their own. Let me illustrate this assertion by two examples, one supplied to us by England, the other by America.

In England the body which calls itself the Social Democratic Federation, and represents at this moment socialism of the more popular kind, began its campaign with a manifesto which was headed with the familiar words, "All wealth is due to labour; therefore to the labourer all wealth is due." This text or motto was followed by certain figures, with regard to the total income of Great Britain, and the manner in which it is at present distributed. Labour was represented as getting less than one-fourth of the whole, and the labourers were informed that if they would but "educate themselves, agitate, and organise," the remaining three-fourths would automatically pass into their possession. This document, it is true, was issued some twenty years ago;[4] but that the form which socialism takes, when addressed to the masses of the population, has not appreciably altered from that day to this, will be made sufficiently clear by the following pertinent fact. Shortly after my arrival in America, in the winter of 1907, the most active disseminator of socialistic literature in New York sent me, by way of a challenge, a new and very spruce volume, which contained the most important of his previous leaflets and articles, collected and republished, and claiming renewed attention. The first of these--and it was signalised by an accompanying advertisement as fundamental--bore the impressive title of, "Why the Working Man should be a Socialist," and the answer to this question is given in the writer's opening words. "You know," he says, addressing any labourer and the street-worker, "or you ought to know, that you alone produce all the good things of life; and you know, or you ought to know, that by so simple a process as that of casting your ballot intelligently you will be able"--to do what? The writer explains himself in language which, except for a difference in his statistics, is almost a verbal repetition of that of his English predecessors. He specifies two sums, one representing the income which each working-man in America would receive were the entire wealth of the country divided equally among the manual labourers; the other representing the income which, on an average, he actually receives as wages; and the writer tells every working man that, by "merely casting his ballot intelligently," he can secure for himself the whole difference between the larger sum and the less.[5]

But the fact that the Marxian doctrine of the all-productivity of labour, and the consequent economic nullity of all other forms of effort, still supplies the main ideas by which popular socialism is vitalised, is shown perhaps even more distinctly by the popular hopes and demands which result from this doctrine indirectly than it is by the direct reassertion of the formal doctrine itself. One of the members of the Parliamentary Labour party in England celebrated his success at the polls by a letter to the Times, proclaiming that socialism was a moral quite as much as an economic movement, and that an object which to socialists was dearer even than the seizure of the riches of the rich, was the achievement of "economic freedom," or, in other words, the "emancipation of labour," or, in other words again, the abolition of the system which he described as "wagedom." I merely mention the particular letter in question in order to remind the reader of these familiar phrases, which are current in every country where the theory of socialism has spread itself.

Now, what does all this talk about the emancipation of labour mean? It can only mean one or other of two things: either that the economic prosperity of every nation in the future will depend on the emancipation of every average mind from the guidance of any minds that are in any way superior to itself, or are able to enhance the productivity of an average pair of hands--a proposition so ludicrous that nobody would consciously assent to it; or else it means a continued assent to the theory which fails to correlate labour with directive ability at all, and so never raises the question of whether the latter is necessary or no.

What, then, becomes of that chorus of vehement protestations, with which my critics in America were all so eager to overwhelm me, to the effect that socialists to-day recognise as clearly as I do that "common manual labour," as Mr. Hillquit puts it, "is impotent to produce the wealth of modern nations," apart from the "organisation and control" of the minds most competent to direct it? That the more intellectual socialists of to-day do recognise this fact-- some with greater and some with less distinctness--is the very point on which I am anxious to insist. We shall have abundant opportunities for considering it later on. For the moment, however, I pause to ask them the following question. Recognising, as they do, and eagerly proclaiming as they do, whenever they address themselves to those who are capable of serious dispute with them, that the original theory of socialism, which was the creed of such bodies as the International, is absolutely false in itself, and in many of the expectations which it stimulates, why do not they set themselves, whenever they address the multitude, to expose and repudiate a fallacy in which they no longer believe? Do they do this? Do they make an attempt to do this? On the contrary, as a rule, though there are doubtless many honourable exceptions, they endeavour to hide from the multitude their intellectual change of front altogether; and, instead of insisting that the undirected labour of the many is, in the modern world, impotent to produce anything, they continue to speak of it as though it produced everything, and as though no class other than the labouring fulfilled any economic function or had any right to exist.[6]

Let me give the reader an example, which is curiously apt here. It is taken from Mr. Hillquit's own attack on myself, which filled the front sheet of a newspaper, and was distributed to the public at the door of one of the buildings in which I spoke. Of the short passages, amounting to some twenty lines out of six hundred, in which alone he condescended to detailed argument, the first is that in which, as we have already seen, he declares that all socialists know, without any instruction on my part, that common manual labour, unless it is directed by ability, is "impotent to produce the wealth of modern nations." But having made this admission with much blowing of trumpets, he immediately drops it, and instead of developing its consequences, he diverts the attention of his readers from it by a long series of irrelevancies; nor does he return to the question of directive ability at all till he is nearing the end of his discourse, when he suddenly takes it up again, declaring that he will meet and refute me on ground which I myself have chosen, and show that wealth--at all events in the commercial sense--is still produced by manual labour alone. He refers to my selection of the case of a printed book, as illustrating, in the manner explained in an earlier chapter, the part which directive ability plays in modern production. The economic value of an edition of a printed book, I said, as the reader will remember, depends in the most obvious way, not on the labour of compositors, but on the quality of the directions which the author imposes on this labour through his manuscript--the author's mind being typical of directive ability generally. And what has Mr. Hillquit--the intellectual Ajax of the socialists--got to say about this? "Whether a book," he says, "is a work of genius or mere rubbish will largely affect its literary or artistic value; but it will have very little bearing on its economic or commercial value." This, he goes on to argue, will, despite all my objections, be found to depend on ordinary manual labour, of which the labour of the hands of the compositors is that which concerns us most. Nothing, according to him, can be more evident than this. "For the market price," he says, "of a wretched detective story, of the same length as Hamlet, and printed in the same way, will be exactly the same as that of a copy of Hamlet itself."

Now, if we consider Mr. Hillquit as a purely literary critic, we can but admire his subtlety in discovering that the literary value of a book is largely affected by the fact of the book's not being rubbish; but when he descends from pure criticism to economics, it is difficult, unless we suppose him to have taken leave of his senses, to imagine that he can himself believe in the medley of nonsense propounded by him. For what he is here doing--or more probably pretending to do--is to confuse the cost of producing an edition of a book with the commercial value of that edition when produced. The labour in question no doubt determines the price at which the printed paper can be sold at a profit, or without loss; but the number of copies which the public will be willing to buy, or, in other words, the value of the edition commercially, depends on qualities resident in the mind of the author, which render the book attractive to but few readers, or to many. Whether these qualities amount to genius in the higher sense of the word, or to nothing more than a knack of titillating the curiosity of the vulgar, does not affect the question. In either case--and this is the sole important fact--they are qualities of the author's mind, and of the author's mind alone; and the labour of the compositors conduces to the production of a pile of volumes which is of large, of little, or of no value commercially, not according to the dexterity with which this labour is performed, but according to the manner in which the author's mind directs it.

Than any human being who is capable of perceiving that the literary quality of a book is largely affected by the fact of the book's not being rubbish, should seriously suppose that the saleable value of editions--whether they are editions of a popular novel, or of a treatise on the conchology of Kamchatka, is proportionate to the number of letters in them arranged in parallel lines--for Mr. Hillquit's argument means neither more nor less than this--is, let me repeat, incredible. What, then, is the explanation of his indulging in a performance of this degrading kind? The explanation is that he, like so many of his colleagues, though recognising personally that labour among "modern nations" depends for its higher productivity on the picked men who direct it, cannot bring himself to renounce, when he is making his appeal to the masses, the old doctrine that they are the sole producers; and accordingly having started with the ostentatious admission that directive ability is as essential to production as labour is, he endeavours by his verbal jugglery with the case of a printed book to convey the impression that labour produces all values after all; and he actually manages to wind up with a repetition of the old Marxian moral that the profits of ability mean nothing but labour which has not been paid for.[7]

One of my reasons, then, for beginning the present examination of socialism with exposing the fallacy of principles which the intellectual socialists of to-day are so eager to proclaim that they have long since abandoned, is the fact that these principles are still the principles of the multitude; that for practical purposes they are those which most urgently require refutation; and that the intellectual socialists who have doubtless repudiated them personally, not only do not attempt to discredit them in the eyes of the ignorant, but themselves continue to appeal to them as instruments of popular agitation.

My other reason for following the course in question is that the theory of socialism in its higher and more recent forms, which recognises directive intellect in addition to manual effort as one of the forces essential to the production of modern wealth, cannot be understood and estimated in any profitable way, without a previous examination of those earlier doctrines and ideas, some of which it still retains, while it modifies and rejects others.

And now let us take up again the thread of our main argument. We laid this down early in the present chapter, having emphasised the fact that, the intellectual socialists of to-day agree, on their own admission, with one proposition at all events which has been elucidated in this volume--namely, that labour alone, as one of their spokesmen puts it, "is impotent to produce the wealth of modern nations," the faculties and the functions of the minority by whom labour is directed and organised being no less essential to the result than the labour of the majority itself. In the following chapter we shall see that this agreement extends yet further.

FOOTNOTES:

[3] Mr. Hillquit--a lawyer, who has adopted the business of propagating socialism in America--is unknown in England; but his name, not long ago, was to be found in the English papers, as that of one of the representatives sent from America to a recent Socialistic Congress in Europe. Amongst the socialists of the United States he holds a position analogous to that enjoyed by Mr. Shaw, Mr. Webb, and Mr. Ramsey Macdonald in England.

[4] Whilst this work was in the press a "Catechism," lately published in England, for use of children, was sent me. It was proposed to use this

Catechism on Sundays in the London County Council Schools. The first economic "lesson" in it begins thus: "Who creates all wealth? The working-class. Who are the workers? Men who work for wages." All who are not wage-workers are declared in this catechism to be absolutely idle and not productive.

[5] The writer of this leaflet, Mr. Wilshire, has subsequently declared in his published criticisms of myself, that I impute to socialists what no socialists really say, and contends that, when he thus speaks of "working-men" and "labourers," he includes all men who contribute anything to the productive forces of a country--inventors like Mr. Edison, and millionaire captains of industry, in so far as they are active agents, and not mere recipients of interest. But that such is not the meaning which he conveys, or desires to convey, to those to whom his leaflet addresses itself, is plainly shown by his statistics, if by nothing else; for the share of the national income, which goes, as he asserts, to "labour," is avowedly the amount which, according to his estimate, is paid to-day in America, as weekly wages to the mass of manual labourers. To say that labour in its more extended sense is the producer of all wealth, is a mere meaningless platitude. It is to say that there would be no wealth without effort of some kind. Does Mr. Wilshire seriously wish us to believe that he is telling Mr. Edison that "if he will only cast his ballot intelligently" he will be able to treble his income at the expense of richer men?

[6] This applies to England no less than to America. Whenever any one of the more educated amongst the socialistic agitators is taxed with maintaining the popular doctrines of socialism with regard to labour, he at once repudiates them, and accuses his opponents of imputing to him and his fellows childish fallacies which no one in his senses would maintain; but the propagation of these fallacies amongst the more ignorant sections of the population continues just the same.

[7] According to Mr. Hillquit, Dickens, for example, made his whole fortune by robbing his compositors.

CHAPTER VI

REPUDIATION OF MARX BY MODERN SOCIALISTS, CONTINUED. THEIR RECOGNITION OF CAPITAL AS THE IMPLEMENT OF DIRECTIVE ABILITY. THEIR

The reader will remember how, having first elucidated the part which exceptional mental faculties, concentrated on the direction of labour, and here called ability, play in modern production, I proceeded to the question of the means by which this direction is accomplished, and showed that these were supplied by the possession of wage-capital--capitalism thus representing no mere passive monopoly, but a system of reins which are attached to innumerable horses, and are useless except as vehicles of the skill with which the coachmen handle them. We shall find that by implication, if not always by direct admission, the intellectual socialists of to-day are in virtual but unacknowledged agreement with this further portion of the present argument also.

In order to demonstrate that such is the case, let me briefly call attention to a point on which we shall have to dwell at much greater length presently-- namely, that these socialists, though they reject the theory of production on which morally and intellectually the earlier socialism based itself, persist in making promises to the labourers precisely of the same kind as those with which the earlier socialism first whetted their appetites. In especial besides promising them indefinitely augmented wealth, they continue to promise them also some sort of _economic emancipation_; and many of these socialists, in explicit accord with their predecessors, declare that what they mean by emancipation is the entire abolition of the wage-system.

Prominent among this number are Mr. Sidney Webb and his colleagues, who are certainly the best educated group of socialistic thinkers in England. Mr. Webb, in particular, is a man of conspicuous talent, and few writers can afford a more favourable illustration than he does of the lines along which the socialistic theory of society is compelled, by the exigencies of logical thought, to develop itself. Now, in proposing to abolish the wage-system, Mr. Webb and his fellow-theorists do not do so without specifying a definite substitute; and when we come to consider what their substitute is, we shall find that it implies, on their part, a full recognition of the function which wage-capital, as the instrument of ability, performs in modern production.

Now, the reader must observe that, in indicating the nature of the function in question--namely, that of providing a means by which the process of direction may be accomplished--and in showing how under the existing system wage-capital is what actually performs it, I never for a moment implied that wage-capital was the only means by which the same result might be accomplished. Indeed, if we look back into the past history of mankind, we shall find that there are two systems other than that of wages, by which the conformity of labour to the requisite directions of ability, not only might be, but actually has been secured. One of these is the corv system prevalent in the Middle Ages. The other system is that of slavery. Under the corv system, peasants were the proprietors of the plots of ground on which they lived, and were thus able to maintain themselves by working at their own discretion; but they were compelled by their tenure to place a certain part of their time at the disposal of their feudal superior, and to work according to his orders. If only a number of otherwise independent peasants could be forced to give enough of their time to the proprietor of a factory to-day, the entire use of wage-capital would in his case be gone. The same thing is true of slavery. Like the peasant proprietor, who gives part of his time to his overlord, the slave is provided with the necessaries of life independently of his obedience to the detailed orders of his master. His master feeds him just as he would feed an animal; the industrial obedience is insured by the subsequent application of force.

These two coercive systems are the only alternatives to the wage-system that have ever been found workable in the past history of the world. We will now consider the system which some of the most thoughtful socialists of to-day are proposing as a substitute for it in the hoped-for socialistic future. The school of English socialists, of which Mr. Webb is the best-known member, have given to the world a volume called Fabian Essays. This volume was republished in America, and to the American edition a special preface was prefixed with a view to emphasising the essentials of a socialistic conception of society, and bringing the details of the socialistic theory up to date. In this preface it is stated, with regard to the apportionment of material wealth generally, that "the only truly socialistic scheme" is one which "will absolutely abolish all economic distinctions, and prevent the possibility of their ever again arising." And how would it accomplish this end? "By making," says the writer, "an equal provision for all an indefeasible condition of citizenship, without any regard whatever to the relative specific services of the different citizens. The rendering of such services on the other hand," the writer goes on, "instead of being left to the option of the citizen, with the alternative of starvation (as is the case under the wage-system) would be secured under one uniform law of civic duty, precisely like other forms of taxation or military service."

Such, then, is the system which is put forward by educated socialists to-day as the only means of escape from the existing system of wages. And an escape from the wage-system--and one not theoretically impracticable--it no doubt is; but an escape into what? It is an escape into one of those systems which I have just now mentioned. That is to say, it is an escape into economic slavery. For the very essence of the position of the slave, as contrasted with the wage-paid labourer, is, so far as the direction of his industrial actions is concerned, that he has not to work as he is bidden in order to gain a livelihood, but that, his livelihood being assured him no matter how he behaves himself, he is obliged to work as he is bidden in order to avoid the lash, or some other form of equally effective punishment.[8]

Now, I am not attempting here to find any fault with socialism on the ground that it would, on the admission of some of its most thoughtful exponents, be obliged to re-establish slavery as the price of emancipation from "wagedom." I have commented on this fact solely with the view to showing that the nature of the alternative to the wage-system thus proposed indicates a full recognition, on the part of those proposing it, of the nature and necessity of the functions which the wage-system performs at present-- namely, that of supplying the means by which the ablest minds in the community secure from the mass of the citizens the punctual performance of the industrial tasks required of them. I am not even insisting that such a slave-system as Mr. Webb contemplates is logically essential to the theory of intellectual socialism at all. On the contrary, as may be seen from a letter addressed to myself by a member of a socialistic body at Chicago, many socialists, as to this matter, are opposed to Mr. Webb altogether. Socialists, says my correspondent, speaking for himself and his associates, have no objection whatever to the system of "wagedom" as such; nor do they wish to see the direction of labour "enforced by the power of the law." They recognise, he says, quoting my own words, that production under socialism, just as under the present system, will be efficient in proportion as labour is directed by the best minds "which can enhance the productivity of an average pair of hands." They object to the wage-system only in so far as it is a means by "which the employing class can make a profit out of the labourers";

and the only change which in this respect socialists desire to introduce is to transfer the business of wage-paying from the private capitalist to the state-- the state which will have no "private interests to serve," and consequently no temptation to appropriate any profits for itself. Socialists, he continues, subject to this proviso, would leave the wage-system just as it is now. The state would pay those who worked, and in accordance with the work they did; but the idle or refractory it would "leave to starve to death, if they so elected, unless somebody wished to keep them alive, as happens at the present time."

The difference between socialists with regard to this question, however, does nothing in itself to discredit the socialistic theory as a whole. It has merely the effect of providing us with two sets of witnesses instead of one to the truth of a common principle, which is recognised by both equally. One set declares that the ability of the most competent men must direct the labours of the majority by means of an appeal to their fears; the other declares that the same result must be accomplished, as it is at the present time, by an appeal to their choice and prudence. In either case it is admitted that the separate manual tasks performed by the majority of the citizens must be directed and co-ordinated by the most competent minds somehow; and that the process of direction must have some system at the back of it, by means of which the orders issued to each labourer can be enforced--this system being either a continuation of that which is in existence now, or another which would to most people be in many ways more distasteful.

The socialists of to-day, in admitting that such is the case, have at last placed themselves in a line with the sober realities of life, and in doing so have assimilated their own analysis of production to the analysis set forth in the beginning of the present volume.

Apart from the fact that, according to their constructive programme, private capitalism would be abolished, and the sole capitalist would be the state, the socialistic system of production, as they have now come to conceive of it, would, in respect of the vital forces involved, be merely the existing system continued under another name, with a directing minority composed of exceptional men on the one hand, and a majority composed of directed men on the other. But in the minds of many socialistic thinkers the simplicity of the situation is obscured by the vagueness of the ideas which they associate with the phrase "the state." For them these ideas are like a fog, into which private capitalism disappears, and in which the forces represented by it lose all definite character. The state, however, is in reality nothing but a collection of individuals; and if the state, besides being a political body, is to become the sole industrial capitalist also, state capitalism, just like private capitalism, will succeed or fail in proportion to the talents of those to whom capital is intrusted as a means of directing the labourers.

If, then, in any capitalistic country, such as Great Britain or America, the business of production could become socialised to-morrow, the best that could possibly happen would be the transformation of the present employers into so many state officials, who industrially would be the state itself. The only difference would be that they would have lost all personal interest in the pecuniary results of the talents which they would still be expected to exercise.[9]

Now, if such a transformation of circumstances could be suddenly effected to-morrow, without any corresponding change in the dispositions of these men themselves, there is theoretically no reason for supposing that the process of production might not continue to be as efficient as it is now, so long as this precise situation lasted. But it could not last. It would be transitory in its very nature. The present generation of industrial directors would die, and in order that the efficiency of the state as the director of labour might be maintained, other men would have to be discovered who were possessed of equal ability in the first place, and who in the second could be trusted or compelled to use it unremittingly to the utmost, in the absence of the main motive which has actuated such men hitherto.

Apart from the problems involved in these two requirements, neither the theory of production which is put forward, nor the productive system which is advocated, by the intellectual socialists of to-day, contains anything with which theoretically the most uncompromising of their opponents could quarrel. It is on these two problems that everything will be found to turn--one being the problem of how, under the conditions which socialism would introduce, the ablest men could be discovered, and invested according to their efficiency with the requisite industrial authority; the other being the problem of how, under the same conditions, it would be possible to secure from such men that full exertion of their talents, on which the material prosperity of the entire community would depend.

For socialists these two problems may be said to be practically new. So long as socialism based itself on the Marxian theory of production, the selection, and the subsequent conduct of the men who would compose the industrial state presented no appreciable difficulties. For the state would, according to this theory, be in no sense the director of the labourers; it would merely be their humble servant. It would be like an old woman who sat all day long in a barn, counting, sorting, and making up into equal shares the different products brought in to her by her sons, who worked out of her sight in a dozen different fields; or, to quote the words of one of my late socialistic correspondents, the functions of the industrial state would be "simply industrial-clerical." The industrial state would consist of clerks and shop-boys, the former of whom added up accounts, while the latter weighed, sorted, and handed out goods over a counter. If the industrial state were to be nothing more than this, the selection of an adequate personnel would doubtless present no difficulties. But as soon as the socialistic theory recognises that the industrial state, instead of being the mere receiver and dispenser of products produced by labour, would represent the intellectual forces by which every process of labour is directed, the problems of how the individuals who compose the state are to be chosen, and of how the continuous exertion of their highest faculties is to be secured, become the fundamental problems which socialists are called upon to consider.

If we assume that under the regime of socialism a nation could always secure, as the official directors of its labour, the men whose ability would enable them to direct it to the best advantage, and could force these men to exert their exceptional faculties to the utmost, the exaction of obedience to their orders from the common labouring citizens, let me say once more, would present no theoretical difficulty. But the task of securing the requisite ability itself is of a wholly different kind. Let us consider why.

Any one armed with an adequate implement of authority, whether the control of the means of subsistence or the power of inflicting punishment, can secure, within limits, from any ordinary man the punctual performance of any ordinary manual task, and the performance of it in a prescribed way; but he is able to do this for the following reasons only: So far as ordinary labour is concerned, any one man, by simply observing another, can tell with approximate accuracy what the other man can do--whether he can trundle a wheel-barrow, hit a nail on the head, file a casting, or lay brick on brick. Further, the director of labour knows the precise nature of the result which he requires in each case that the individual labourer shall accomplish. Hence he can exact from each labourer conformity to the injunctions laid on him, in respect both of the general character and the particular application of his efforts. But in respect of the faculties distinctive of those exceptional men by whom alone ordinary labour can be directed to the best advantage, both these conditions are wanting. It is impossible to tell that any man of ability possesses any exceptional faculties for directing labour at all, unless he himself chooses to show them; and, indeed, until circumstances supply him with some motive for showing them, he may very well not be aware that he possesses such faculties himself. Moreover, even if he gives the world some reason to suspect their existence, the world at large will not know what he can do with them, and will consequently be unable to impose on him any definite task. A pressgang could have forced Columbus to labour as a common seaman; but not all the population of Europe could have forced him to discover a world beyond the Atlantic; for the mass of his contemporaries, until his enterprise proved successful, obstinately refused to believe that there was such a world to discover.

The men, therefore, on the exercise of whose directive ability the productive efficiency of a modern nation depends, would occupy, with regard to any nation organised on socialistic principles, a position fundamentally different from that of the ordinary labourer. The exercise of their distinctive powers, unlike those of the labourer, could never be secured by coercion; because neither the nation at large, nor any body of representatives, could possibly know that these powers existed until the possessors of them chose to reveal the secret. They could not be made to reveal it. They could only be induced to do so; and they could only be induced to do so by a society which was so constituted as to offer for an exceptional performance some exceptional reward, just as a reward is offered for evidence against an unknown murderer. The reward at present offered them is the possession of some exceptional share of the wealth to the production of which their efforts have exceptionally contributed; and, hence, since it is the object of all socialistic schemes to render the achievement of such a reward impossible, we shall find that the ultimate problem for socialists of the modern school is how to discover another which in practice will be equally efficacious.

But though this is the ultimate problem, it is very far from being the only one which the theory of socialism in its modern form raises. Directive ability, which is a compound of many faculties, varies greatly in degree and kind. Its value, if tested by the results of its actual application to labour, would in some cases be immense, in other cases very small, and in others it would be a minus quantity. Thus, even if we suppose that the exercise of it is so far its own reward that all who believe themselves to possess it--and these are a very large number--will, for the mere pleasure of exercising it, be eager to gain the positions which will make its exercise possible, the problem would remain of how to discriminate those who would, as industrial directors, achieve the greatest successes, from those who would bring about nothing but relative or absolute failure. This problem of how, under a regime of socialism, ability could be so tested that the practical means of direction could be granted to or withheld from it, according to its actual efficiency, is the problem which we will consider first; for though of secondary importance as compared with the problem of motive, it is in more immediate connection with the details of daily business.

FOOTNOTES:

[8] The economic condition of the great mass of the population, which this "up-to-date" socialist contemplates, is precisely analogous to that of the Helots in Sparta, whose subsistence was secured independently of their specific services, whilst their services to the directing class were wrung from them by a system of iron discipline.

[9] While these pages were in the hands of the printers, a work was published by an American socialist, in which it is asserted that the socialisation of America would consist at first of this precise process--namely, the conversion of all the existing active employers and directors of labour into the salaried servants of some state department.

CHAPTER VII

PROXIMATE DIFFICULTIES. ABLE MEN AS A CORPORATION OF STATE OFFICIALS

For the moment, then, we will waive the problem of motive altogether; we will assume that a society which denied to its able men any pecuniary reward proportionate to the magnitude of its products could provide them with a motive of some kind--we need not inquire what--which would prompt them still to exert themselves as eagerly as they do now; and we will merely consider how, a multitude of such men being given, the most efficient of them could be constantly selected as the official directors of labour, and the rest, in proportion to their inefficiency, be either dismissed or excluded. In order to realise the difficulties which, in this respect, socialism would have to face, let us consider the manner in which the problem is solved now.

Under the system of private capitalism it solves itself by an automatic process. In order that any man may direct the labour of other men, he must, under that system, be the possessor or controller of so much wage-capital. Now this capital--this implement of direction--in proportion as it is employed, disappears, and is reproduced only by a subsequent sale of the products resulting from the labour in the direction of which it has been expended. Thus a man, we will say, invents a new engine for motor-cars, and devotes to the production of twenty engines of the kind all the capital which he possesses--namely, two thousand guineas. Apart from the raw material out of which the engines are to be constructed, his whole expenditure will consist in paying wages to certain labourers, on condition that they work up this metal in a manner which he prescribes to them. For the raw metal he pays, we will say, a hundred pounds, or the odd shillings of the guineas. He pays to twenty labourers a hundred pounds apiece as wages; and the result is twenty engines. If the engines are successful, and if the public will give him a hundred and fifty guineas for each of them, the man has got his entire capital back again, with a thousand guineas added to it, and can continue his direction of labour by means of wages, on the same lines, and on a much more extended scale. But if the engines, when tried, develop some inherent defect, and he consequently can sell none of them, he may still, perhaps, get back the price of the raw metal--a petty sum, insufficient for his own needs-- but his whole wage-capital will be gone, and with it his power of directing any further labour in the future. In other words, under the system of private capitalism, if labour has been directed by any man in an unsuccessful way, the resulting products being such that nobody cares to buy them, or in exact proportion as this result is approached, the man's implement of direction passes out of his hands altogether; and the simple fact of his having directed labour ill deprives him of the means of directing or of misdirecting it again.

But under a system of state socialism the situation would be wholly changed. Private capitalism is, in this respect, self-acting, and acts with absolute accuracy, because wage-capital being divided into a multitude of independent reservoirs, its waste at any one point brings about its own remedy. Each reservoir is like a mill-pond which automatically begins to dry up whenever its contents are employed in actuating a useless mill; and the man who has wasted his water is able to waste no more. But the moment the divisions between the reservoirs are broken down, and the separate capitals contained in them become, as would be the case under socialism, fused together like the waters of a single lake, the director of labour who so misused any portion of this fluid stock that the products of labour, as directed by him, failed to replace the wages, would not thereby be incapacitated from continuing his misdirections further; for the wage-capital dissipated by his incompetence could, under these conditions, always be replaced, and its loss more or less concealed, by fresh supplies which had a really different origin. It was only in consequence of conditions resembling these that the London County Council was enabled to continue for so long its service of Thames steamboats, in spite of the fact that the labour thus employed failed to reproduce, by the functions which it performed for the public, more than a fraction of capital which was necessarily consumed in its maintenance. Had labour been thus misdirected by any private capitalist, his misdirection of it would have soon been checked by his loss of the means of continuing it; but the County Council, with the purse of the community at its back, was able, by taxing the industrial successes of others, to refinance and prolong its own industrial failure.

Socialists wholly overlook the importance of these considerations. Many of them, for example, in the case of the London County Council's steamboats, defended that enterprise in spite of its financial failure, on the ground that the steamboats were a convenience to certain travellers at all events, who in all probability were persons of modest means, while the loss would be made good out of the pockets of the ratepayers who were presumably rich. But even if this argument were plausible as applied to a state of society in which the incomes of some men were greater than those of others, it would be absolutely inapplicable to conditions such as those desired by socialists, under which the incomes of all would be fractions, approximately equal, of a common stock to the production of which all contributed. For it must surely be apparent to even the meanest intelligence that whatever diminished the aggregate amount to be divided would diminish the fraction of it which falls to the share of each; and it ought to be equally apparent, though to many people it is not, that the labour of any labourer which is directed in such a way that the men consume more articles of utility than they produce, or fail to produce as many as they would do if directed better, has this precise effect of diminishing the divisible total, by making it either less than it has been or less than it would be otherwise.[10]

Thus, in cases such as that of the London County Council's steamboats, the efficiency of labour is so lessened by incompetent direction that the labourers employed can only perform for society one-half of the services which society must perform for them. For every hour which they spend in conveying ten men on the river, twenty men must work to provide them with food and clothing. So long as fortunes are unequal, and depend on individual effort and enterprise, such losses may be localised and obscured in a hundred different ways; but the moment all fortunes, as they would be under the regime of socialism, were reduced to specific fractions of the aggregate product of the community, any decline in the efficiency of the labour of any single group would result in a diminution of the income of every member of all the others. Wherever ten men were employed to do what might have been done by nine, the contribution to the general stock would be less by ten per cent. than it might have been. If ten men were employed in making chairs, which might have been made by nine had their labour been better directed, the community would lose the cushions which in that case would have been made by the tenth. And what holds good of labour in respect of its productive efficiency holds good of it also in respect of the character of the goods produced. If ten men were employed in producing forty loaves when all that could be eaten was twenty, not only would the remaining twenty be wasted, but the community would lose the butter which might have been made instead of them. The importance, therefore, to the community as a whole of having every branch of its labour directed by those men, and by those men only, whose ability would raise it to the highest pitch of efficiency, and cause it to produce only such goods and such quantities of them as would satisfy from moment to moment the needs and tastes of the population, would, under a regime of socialism, be even more general and immediate than it is at the present day; and yet at the same time, for reasons to which we will now return, the difficulty of securing the requisite ability would be increased.

It is impossible to illustrate in detail the situation which would thus arise; for the state, as sole capitalist and sole director of labour, is an institution which imaginably might take various forms; and socialists, in this case exhibiting a commendable prudence, have refrained from committing themselves to any detailed programme. The socialistic state, however, having to perform a double function--namely, that of political governor and universal director of industry--would necessarily be divided into two distinct bodies. One of these, consisting of statesmen and legislators, would, we may assume, be elected by the votes of the people. But the other, consisting of industrial experts--the inventors, the chemists, the electricians, the naval engineers, the organisers of labour--might conceivably be in the first or the second of the two following positions: They might either be left free, as they are under the existing system, to do severally the best they can, according to their own lights, in estimating what goods or services the population wants, and in satisfying these wants with such increasing economy that new goods and services might be continually added to the old. They might be left free to promote or dismiss subordinates, to fill up vacancies, and take new men into partnership, very much as the heads of private firms do now. Or else they might be liable, in greater or less degree, to removal or supersession, and interference with their technical operations, on the part of the political body, whose members, while representing the general ideas of the community, would presumably not be experts in the direction of its particular industries.

Now, let us suppose first that the official directors of labour are left practically free to follow their own devices. The situation which will arise may be illustrated by the following imaginary case: The nation, let us say, requires two sister ships. They are built in different yards, under two different directors, and a thousand labourers are employed in the construction of each; but while the labourers who work under one director take a year to complete their task, those who work under the other complete theirs within ten months. This would mean for the community that, through the inferiority of the former of these two officials, two months' labour of the national shipwrights had been lost; and the public interest would require that the industrial regiment commanded by him should as quickly as possible pass out of his control into that of an official who could render it more efficient than he. And under the existing system this, as we have seen already, is precisely what sooner or later would be brought about automatically. The inefficient director, in proportion to his relative inefficiency, loses his customers, and can direct labour no longer, or is obliged to direct it on a very much reduced scale. But if each director of labour owed, as he would do under socialism, his means of directing it, not to the results of his individual efficiency, but to a single common source--namely, to the collective capital of the country or the forcible authority of the law--there is nothing in the fact that one constructor of ships wastes labour in constructing them which another constructor would have saved, to prevent him from continuing in his post, or even to insure that he will vacate it in favour of an abler man, whether an official rival or otherwise, as soon as such a man is available.

There is also this further fact to be noted. Although we are assuming that the socialistic directors of labour will exert their talents to the utmost without requiring the stimulus of a proportionate reward in money, we must necessarily assume that they will value their posts for some reason or other just as much as they would do were the largest emoluments attached to them. Consequently we may, condescending to vulgar language, say, as a certainty, that they will do their very best to stick to them. All these official persons, as contrasted with the labouring public, will occupy positions of similar and desirable privilege; and while their latent rivalry among themselves will be hampered in the manner just indicated, they will none of them be inclined to welcome any further rivalry from without. If the least efficient of our two naval constructors could not be forced by the fact of his relative inefficiency to hand over all or any portion of his authority to the other, and would certainly not be likely to do so of his own free will, it is still less likely that either would be willing to make such a sacrifice in favour of a man outside the privileged ranks, who desired an opportunity of demonstrating his practical superiority to both.

Under a system, in short, like that which we are now contemplating, the ability of the ablest directors might, in each branch of industry, raise the efficiency of the labour directed by themselves to as high a pitch as that to which it could be raised by the competition of to-day. But the successes of the ablest men would have no tendency to self-extension. The ablest men would do better than the less able, but would have no tendency to displace them; and the ablest and the least able members of the industrial oligarchy alike would instinctively oppose, and would also be in a position to check, the practical development of any competition from without.

That this is no fanciful estimate can be shown by an appeal to facts. We may take as an example the case of the British post-office. The inefficient transmission of letters some twenty years ago in London provoked an effort to supplement it by a service of private messengers. The post-office authorities were instantly up in arms, ready to nip this enterprise in the bud, and forcibly prevent any other human being from doing what they were still, to all appearance, determined not to do themselves.[11] Then, as a grudging concession, permission to transmit letters with a promptitude which the post-office still declined to emulate was accorded to a company on condition that for each letter carrier the post-office should be paid as it would have been had it carried the letter itself; and thus there was established at last the institution of the Boy Messengers.

Similar examples are afforded by the conduct of the state in France, where the manufacture of tobacco and matches are both of them state monopolies. To say that the tobacco produced by the French state is unsmokable, and that the matches produced by it will not light a candle, would no doubt be an exaggeration; but they are both inferior to the products which private enterprise could, if left to itself, produce at the same price. And private enterprise is, indeed, not wholly suppressed. Excellent tobacco and matches, both of private manufacture, are allowed to be sold in France; but the producers of both are artificially handicapped by having to pay to the state, on every box or every pound sold, either the whole or part of the profit which the state itself would have made by selling an equal quantity of its own inferior articles.

The very fact, indeed, that the state, as a producer, or a renderer of public services, such as letter-carrying, has thus to protect itself against the competition of private enterprise, is sufficient evidence of the difficulties which a state organisation encounters in securing industrial ability which shall be constantly of the highest kind, and also of its inevitable tendency to hamper, if not to stifle, the development and the practical activity of superior ability elsewhere. And if these difficulties and this tendency are appreciable in state-directed industries now, when the area of direction is small and strictly limited, the reader may easily imagine how incalculably more formidable they would become if extended, as socialism would extend them, to the activities of the entire community.

We have thus far been considering the position of the directors of socialised industry on the assumption that they would be free to follow the dictates of their own several intelligences, without any technical interference from officials of any other kind. Let us now consider the alternative which, in any socialistic society, would most closely coincide with fact. This is the assumption that the official directors of labour would not be technical autocrats, but would be subject to the control of their brother officials, the statesmen, who represented the great mass of the people.

Now, no doubt the intervention of a body of this kind might obviate some of the difficulties on which we have just been dwelling. It might lead to the removal of some directors of labour who were not only relatively inefficient, but were positively and notoriously mischievous; but it would introduce difficulties greater than those it obviated. For while the industrial officials would, in exact proportion to their efficiency, embody the special expertness peculiar to a gifted few, the political officials, in proportion as they represented their electorate, would embody the preponderating opinions and the general intelligence of the many. The political officials, therefore, could, from the very nature of the case, never represent any ideas or condition of knowledge which appreciably transcended or conflicted with those of the least intelligent; and the logical result would be that no industrial improvements could in a socialistic community be initiated by the highest intelligence, if they went beyond what could be apprehended and consciously approved of by the lowest.

And here again, though our estimate is only general and speculative--for it deals with a state of things which at present has no existence--we can turn to historical facts for illustrations of its substantial truth. For example, if in the days of Columbus all the capital of Europe and the control of its entire labour had been vested in a government which represented the all but universal opinion of all the western nations, the discovery of America would have obviously been beyond the limits of possibility. It was rendered possible only because Columbus secured two patrons who, resembling in this respect far-seeing investors of to-day, dared to be original, and provided him with the necessary ships and control over the necessary labour. Or let us take the case of the iron industry of the modern world. This industry, in its vast modern developments, depends entirely on the discovery made in England of a method by which iron might be smelted with coal in place of wood. The completed discovery was due to a succession of solitary men, beginning with Dud Dudley in the reign of James I., and ending a century later with Darby of Coalbrookdale. Practically these heroic men had all their contemporaries against them. Public opinion attacked them through private persecution and violence. The apathy and vacillation of governments left them without defence; and had governments then represented public opinion completely, and had also controlled all labour and capital, the discovery in question, which was retarded for three generations, would in all probability have never been made at all. Arkwright's experience with regard to his spinning-frame was similar. His epoch-making invention was in danger of being altogether lost, because the general opinion of the capitalists of his day was against it; and if all capital had been vested in a representative state, to the exclusion of the far-seeing individuals who eventually came to his assistance, its loss would have been almost certain. The successful development of the automobile did not take place till yesterday--and why? A steam-driven vehicle ran in Cornwall before the end of the eighteenth century; but the state and public opinion both condemned it as dangerous; and all further progress in the matter was checked for more than twenty years. Then again private enterprise asserted itself, but only to suffer precisely the same fate. Steam-driven omnibuses plied between Paddington and Westminster. Steam-driven stage-coaches plied on the Bath road. But the state and public opinion were again in obstinate opposition; these vehicles were crushed out of existence by the imposition of monstrous tolls; and progress was checked a second time and for a longer period still. An instance yet more modern is that supplied by the electric lighting of London. The electric lighting of London was retarded for ten years solely by the attitude which the state assumed towards private enterprise.

It is needless to multiply illustrations of this kind further; for my object is not to show that the state, as it exists at present, is necessarily inimical to private enterprise as a whole. It is not, for it has not the power to be. But the fact that even now, when its powers are so strictly limited and its points of direct contact with industrial enterprise are so few, tendencies of the kind develop themselves with such marked practical consequences is enough to show the reality and magnitude of the evils which would ensue if a body, which reflected on the one hand the opinions of the average many, and on the other the individual ability of a few, specially privileged and pledged to their own methods, were the sole controller of all manual labour whatsoever, the virtual owner of all the implements which exist at present, the sole determiner of the forms which such implements shall assume in the future, and also of the kinds and quantities of the consumable goods which the implements and the labourers together shall from day to day produce.

But the nature and scope of the effects which would be incident to any general absorption, such as that contemplated by socialists, of productive enterprise by the state, will be yet more clearly seen if we turn to a kind of production on which I have dwelt already, as affording the simplest and most luminous example possible of the respective parts played in the modern world by ordinary manual labour and the exceptional ability which directs it. This is the case of books, or of other printed publications. Many years ago the English radical Charles Bradlaugh urged in a debate with a then prominent socialist that under socialism no literary expression of free thought would be practicable, and I cannot do more than accentuate his lucid and unanswerable arguments. The state, being controller of all the implements of production, a private press would be as illegal as the dies used by a forger. Nobody could issue a book, a newspaper, or even a leaflet, unless the use of a state press were allowed him by the state authorities, together with the disposal of the labour of the requisite number of compositors. Now, it is clear that the state could not bind itself to put presses and compositors at the service of every one of its citizens who was anxious to see himself in print. There would have to be selection and rejection of some drastic kind. The state would have to act as universal publisher's reader. What would happen under these circumstances to purely imaginative literature we need not here inquire; but when the question was one of expressing controversial opinions as to science, religion, morals, and especially social politics, what would happen is evident. The state would be able to refuse, and it could not do otherwise than refuse, to print anything which expressed opinions out of harmony with those which were predominant among its own members. In so far as these members reflected the opinions of the majority, they would never publish an attack on errors which they themselves accepted as vital truths. In so far as they owed their positions to certain real or supposed superiorities they would never publish any criticism of their own methods by men whom they would necessarily regard as mischievous and mistaken inferiors. In short, whether the state acted in this matter as the ultra-superior person, or as the ultra-popular person, the result would be just the same. The focalised prejudices of the majority, or the privileged self-confidence of a certain select minority, would deprive independent thought in any other quarter of any means of expressing itself either by book or journal, and by thus depriving it of its voice would place it at an artificial disadvantage more effectual as a means of repression than the dungeons of the Inquisition itself. It would be checked as completely as the higher criticism of the Bible would have been if the only printer in the whole world were the Pope and the only publishing business were managed by the College of Cardinals.

And what, under a regime of socialism, would be true of human thought, a-seeking to embody itself in printed books or newspapers, would be equally true of it as applied to the methods of industry, and seeking to embody itself in multiplied or improved commodities.

Such, then, are the disadvantages which socialism, as contrasted with the existing system, would introduce in connection with the problem of how to detect, and how, having detected it, to invest with suitable powers, the men whose ability is, at any given moment, calculated to raise labour to the highest pitch of productiveness--how to give power to these, and to take it away from others in exact proportion as their talents, as exhibited in its practical results, fall short of the maximum which is at the time obtainable.

This problem, as we have seen already, the existing system solves by its machinery of private competition, and of independent capitals, which automatically increase the powers of the ablest directors of labour, and concurrently decrease or extinguish those of the less able. Socialism, with its collective capital, and its able men reduced or elevated to the rank of state officials, while not obviating, but on the contrary emphasising the necessity for placing labour under the highest directive ability, or, in other words, the necessity for competition among able men, would dislocate the only machinery by which such competition can be made effective; and, if it did not destroy the efficiency of the highest ability altogether, would reduce this to a minimum, and confine it within the narrowest limits.

In this chapter, however, we have been dealing with the machinery only. We have been assuming the unabated activity of the powers by which the machinery is to be driven. That is to say, we have been assuming that every man who possesses, or imagines himself to possess, any exceptional gift for directing labour--whether as an inventor, a man of science, an organiser, or in any other capacity--would be no less eager, under the circumstances with which socialism would surround him, to develop and exert his faculties than he is at the present day. We will now pass on to the question of how far this assumption is correct. The question of machinery is secondary. It is a question of detail only; for if there is no power in the background by which the machinery may be driven, it will not make much difference in the result whether the machinery be bad or good.

And here once more we shall find that the socialists of to-day agree with us; and in passing on to the question now before us, we shall be quitting a region of speculations which can be only of a general kind (for they refer to social arrangements whose details are not definitely specified), and we shall find ourselves confronted by a variety of ideas and principles which, however confused they may be in the minds of those who enunciate them, we shall have no difficulty ourselves in reducing to logical order.

FOOTNOTES:

[10] That such is the case can be seen easily enough by imagining a socialistic community consisting of twenty men, who require and consume only one article, bread. Each man, to keep him alive, requires one loaf daily; but to eat two would be a comfort to him, and to eat three would be luxury. The community is divided into two groups of ten men each, one man in each group directing the labour of the others. We will start with supposing that these two directors are men of equal and also of the highest ability, and that each of the groups, under these favourable conditions, is enabled to produce daily an output of thirty loaves. The total output of both in this case amounts to sixty, which equally divided yields to everybody the luxurious number of three. Let us next suppose that the director of one group dies, that his place is taken by a man of inferior powers, and that this group, as a consequence of his less efficient direction, instead of producing thirty loaves can produce no more than ten. Now, although this falling off in production has occurred in one group only, the loss which results from it is felt by the entire community. The total output has sunk from sixty loaves to forty; and the members of the group which retains its old efficiency, no less than those of the group which has lost so much of it, have to be content, with a dividend, not of three loaves, but two. Finally, let us suppose that, owing to a continued deterioration in

management, the ten men of whom the first group is composed are able to produce daily, not ten loaves, but only five. That is to say, the number of loaves which they produce comes to no more than half of the minimum they are obliged to eat. Here it is obvious that, unless one-half of the population is to die, it can only be kept alive by being given a supply of loaves which, in consequence of its own inefficiency, must be taken out of the mouths of others.

[11] A similar drama enacted itself in London more than two centuries ago. Private enterprise established a penny post. The state killed it, and deprived the metropolis of this service for a hundred and fifty years.

CHAPTER VIII

THE ULTIMATE DIFFICULTY. SPECULATIVE ATTEMPTS TO MINIMISE IT

When socialism, says Mr. Sidney Webb, shall have abolished all other monopolies, there will still remain to be dealt with the most formidable monopoly of all--namely, "the natural monopoly of business ability," or "the special ability and energy with which some persons are born." The services of these monopolists, he sees and fully admits, would be as essential to a socialistic as they are to any other community which desires to prosper according to modern standards. He sees and admits also that these exceptional men will not continuously exert or even develop their talents unless society can supply them with some adequate motive or stimulus. Accordingly, since he maintains that no scheme of society would be socialistic in any practical sense which did not completely, or at least approximately, eliminate the motive mainly operative among such men at present--namely, that supplied by the possibility of exceptional economic gain--he fairly faces the fact that some motive of a different kind will have to be discovered by socialists which shall take the place of this.

I mention Mr. Webb in particular merely because he represents the views which all intellectual socialists are coming to hold likewise. This specific problem of how to provide the natural monopolists of business ability with all adequate motive to develop and exercise their talents is engaging more and more the attention of the higher socialistic thinkers; and if we take together the passages in their writings which deal with it, it has by this time a voluminous literature of its own.

We shall find that the arguments brought forward by them in this connection divide themselves broadly into two classes, one of which deals with the problem of motive directly, while the other class aims at preparing the way to its solution by showing in advance that its difficulties are far less formidable than they appear to be. Without insisting on the manner in which they are urged by individual writers, we will take these two classes of argument in the logical order which they assume when we consider their general character.

These preparatory arguments, with which we will accordingly begin, while admitting that some men are undoubtedly more able than others, aim at showing that the superiority of such men to their fellows is not so great as it seems to be, and that any claims made by them to exceptional reward on account of it consequently tend to reduce themselves to very modest proportions.

These arguments possess a peculiar interest owing to the fact that they have not originated with socialistic thinkers at all, but have been drawn by them from the evolutionary philosophy of the nineteenth century generally, in so far as it was applied to historical and sociological questions. The dominant idea which distinguished this school of thought was the insignificance of the individual as compared with society past and present. Thus Herbert Spencer, who was its most systematic exponent, opens his work on the Study of Sociology with an elaborate attack on what he calls "The Great Man Theory," according to which the explanation of the main events of history is to be sought in the influence of exceptional or great men--the men who, in vulgar language, are spoken of as "historical characters." Such an explanation, said Spencer, is no explanation at all. Great men, however great, are not isolated phenomena. Whatever they may do as the "proximate initiators" of change, they themselves "have their chief cause in the generations they have descended from," and depend for the influence which is commonly attributed to their actions, on "the multitudinous conditions" of the generation to which they belong. Thus Laplace, he says, could not have got far with his calculations if it had not been for the line of mathematicians who went before him. C鍹ar could not have got very far with his conquests if a great military organisation had not been ready to his hand; nor could Shakespeare have written his dramas if he had not lived in a country already enriched with traditions and a highly developed language.

But though it was Herbert Spencer who invested these arguments with their most systematic form, and gave them their definite place in the theory of evolution as a whole, they were widely diffused already among his immediate predecessors, as we may see by the following passage taken from an unlikely quarter. "It is," says Macaulay, in his Essay on Dryden, anticipating the exact phraseology of Spencer, "the age that makes the man, not the man that makes the age.... The inequalities of the intellect, like the inequalities of the surface of the globe, bear so small a proportion to the mass, that in calculating its great revolutions they may safely be neglected." And Macaulay is merely expressing a doctrine distinctive of his time--a doctrine which, to take one further example, dominated in a notable way the entire thought of Buckle. This doctrine, which, to a greater or less degree, merges the organism in its environment, or the individual, however great, in society, has been seized on by the more recent socialists just as the theory of Ricardo, with regard to labour and value, was seized on by Karl Marx, and has been adapted by them to their own purposes.

Thus Mr. Bellamy, whose book, Looking Backward, descriptive of a socialistic Utopia, achieved a circulation beyond that of the most popular novels, declares that "nine hundred and ninety-nine parts out of the thousand of the produce of every man are the result of his social inheritance and environment"; and Mr. Kidd, a socialist in sentiment if not in definite theory, urges that the comparative insignificance, the comparative commonness, and dependence for their efficiency on contemporary social circumstances, of the talents which we are accustomed to associate with the greatest inventions and discoveries, is proved by the fact that some of the most important of these have been made by persons who, "working quite independently, have arrived at like results almost simultaneously. Thus rival and independent claims," he proceeds, "have been made for the discovery of the differential calculus, the invention of the steam-engine, the methods of spectrum analysis, the telephone, the telegraph, as well as many other discoveries." Further, to these arguments a yet more definite point has been added by the contention that, as socialist writers put it, "inventions and discoveries, when once made, become common property," the mass of mankind being cut off from the use of them only by patents or other artificial restrictions.

The aim of socialists in pursuing this line of reasoning is obvious. It is to demonstrate, or rather to suggest, that "the monopolists of business ability," in spite of their comparative rarity and the importance of the services performed by them, are far from being so rare or so superior to the mass of their contemporaries as they seem to be, that their achievements owe far more than appears on the surface to the co-operation of the average members of society, and that consequently a socialistic society could justly demand and practically secure their services on far easier terms than those which they command at present.

And to such a conclusion the principles of modern evolutionary sociology, as unanimously interpreted by the philosophers of the nineteenth century, may be fairly said to lend the entire weight of their prestige. Let us, then, consider more carefully what these principles are, with a view to understanding the true scope of their significance. We shall find that, although undoubtedly true in themselves, the scope of their significance has been very imperfectly understood by the great thinkers to whose talents their elucidation has been due; that these thinkers, in their eagerness to establish a new truth, have at the same time introduced a new confusion; and that it is from the confusion of a truth with a falsehood, rather than from the truth itself, that the socialists of to-day have been here drawing their inspiration.

The confusion in question arises from a failure to see that sociology is concerned with two distinct sets of phenomena, or with one set regarded from two absolutely distinct standpoints. Thus it is constantly said that man, in the course of ages, has developed civilised societies and the various arts of life--that, beginning as an animal only a little higher than the monkey, he gradually became a builder of cities, a master of the secrets of nature, a philosopher, a poet, a painter of divine pictures. And from a certain point of view this language is adequate. If what we desire to do is to estimate, as speculative philosophers, the significance of the human race in relation to the universe or its Author, by considering its origin on this planet, and its subsequent fortunes hitherto, what interests us is man in the mass, or societies, and not individuals. But if we are interested in any problem of practical life--such, for example, as how to cure cancer, or cut a navigable canal through a broad and mountainous isthmus, or decorate a public building with a series of great frescoes--the central point of interest is the individual and not society. How would a mother, whose child was hovering between life and death, be comforted by the information that man was a great physician? How would America be helped in the construction of the Panama Canal by learning from sociologists that man could remove mountains? How could great pictures be secured for a public building by information to the effect that the greatest of all great artists depended for their exceptional power on the aggregate of conditions surrounding them, when ten millions of men whose surrounding conditions were similar might be tried in succession without one being found who rose in art above the level of vulgar mediocrity? It is not that the generalisations of the evolutionary sociologists with regard to man in the mass, or societies, are untrue philosophically. Philosophically they are of the utmost moment. It is that they have no bearing on the problems of contemporary life, and that they miss out the one factor by which they are brought into connection with it.

Let us take, for example, the way in which Herbert Spencer illustrates the general theorem of the evolutionary sociologists by the case of Shakespeare, and Shakespeare's debt to his times. "Given a Shakespeare," he says, "and what dramas could he have written without the multitudinous conditions of civilised life around him--without the various traditions which, descending to him from the past, gave wealth to his thought, and without the language which a hundred generations had developed and enriched by use?" The answer to this question is to be found in the counter-question that is provoked by it. Given the conditions of civilised life, and the traditions of England and its language, as they were under Queen Elizabeth, how could these have produced the Shakespearian dramas unless England had possessed an individual citizen whose psycho-physical organisation was equal to that of Shakespeare? Similarly, it is true that Turner could not have painted his sunsets if multitudinous atmospheric conditions had not given him sunsets to paint; but at the same time every one of Turner's contemporaries were surrounded by sunsets of precisely the same kind, and yet only Turner was capable of producing such masterpieces as his own. The case of the writer and the artist, indeed, illustrates with singular lucidity the fact which the philosophy of the evolutionary sociologists ignores that the great man does great things, not in virtue of conditions which he shares with the dullest and the feeblest of the men around him, but in virtue of the manner in which his exceptional genius assimilates the data of his environment, and gives them back to the world, recombined, refashioned, and reinterpreted.

And with regard to practical matters, and more especially the modern production of wealth, the case is just the same. No one has illustrated more luminously than Herbert Spencer himself the multitudinous character of the knowledge which modern production necessitates; and no one has insisted with more emphasis than he that one of the rarest faculties to be met with among human beings is the faculty, as he expresses it, of "apprehending assembled propositions in their totality." It would be difficult to define better in equally brief language the intellectual aspect of that composite mental equipment which distinguishes from ordinary men the monopolists of business ability. It is precisely by apprehending a multitude of assembled propositions in their totality--mathematical, chemical, geological, geographical, and so forth--by combining them for a definite purpose, and translating them into a series of orders which organised labour can execute, that the intellect of the able man gives efficiency to the industrial processes of to-day. In addition, moreover, to his purely intellectual faculties, he requires others which, in their higher developments, are no less rare--namely, a quick discernment of popular wants as they arise or an imagination which enables him to anticipate them, an instinctive insight into character which enables him to choose best men as his subordinates, promptitude to seize on opportunities, courage which is the soul of promptitude, and finally a driving energy by which the whole of his moral and intellectual mechanism is actuated. As for "the aggregate of conditions out of which he has arisen," or the aggregate of conditions which surround him, these are common to him and to every one of his fellow-countrymen. They are a landscape which surrounds them all. But aggregates of conditions could no more produce the results of which, as Herbert Spencer admits, the able man is the proximate cause, unless the able man existed and could be induced to cause them, than a landscape could be photographed without a lens or a camera, or a great picture of it painted in the absence of a great artist.

Herbert Spencer, indeed, partially perceives all this himself. That is to say, he realises from time to time that the causal importance of the great man varies according to the nature of the problems in connection with which we consider him and that while he is, for purposes of general speculation, merely a transmitter of forces beyond and greater than himself, he is for practical purposes an ultimate cause or fact. That such is the case is shown in a curiously vivid way by two references to two great men in particular, which occur not far from each other in Spencer's Study of Sociology. One is a reference to the last Napoleon, the other is a reference to the first. He refers to the former when he is emphasising his main proposition, that the importance of the ruler, considered as an individual, is small, and almost entirely merged in the conditions of society generally. "If you wish," he says, "to understand the phenomena of social evolution, you will not do it should you read yourself blind over the biographies of all the great rulers on record, down to Frederick the greedy and Louis Napoleon the treacherous." When he makes his reference to Louis Napoleon's ancestor, he is pausing for a moment in the course of his philosophical argument in order to indulge in a parenthetical denunciation of war. Of the insane folly of war, he says, we can have no better example than that provided by Europe at the beginning of the nineteenth century, when hardly a country was free from "slaughter, suffering, and devastation." For what, he goes on to ask, was the cause of such wide-spread horrors? Simply, he answers, the presence of one abnormal individual, "in whom the instincts of the savage were scarcely at all qualified by what we call moral sentiments"; and "all this slaughter, suffering, and devastation" were, he says, "gone through because one man had a restless desire to be despot over all men." Here we see how Spencer, as a matter of common-sense, instinctively assigns to great men absolutely contrasted positions, according to the point of view from which he is himself regarding them--that of the speculative thinker and that of the practical politician, and of this fact we will take one example more. Of his doctrine that the great man is merely a "proximate initiator," and in no true sense the cause of what he seems to produce or do, he gives us an elaborate illustration taken from modern industry--that is to say, the invention of the Times printing-press. This wonderful piece of mechanism would, he says, have been wholly impossible if it had not been for a series of discoveries and inventions that had gone before it; and having specified a multitude of these, winds up with a repetition of his moral that of each invention individually the true cause is not the so-called inventor, but "the aggregate of conditions out of which he has arisen." But when elsewhere, in his treatise on Social Statics, Spencer is dealing with the existing laws of England, he violently attacks these, in so far as they relate to patents, because they fail, he says, to recognise as absolute a man's "property in his own ideas," or, in other words, "his inventions, which he has wrought, as it were, out of the very substance of his own mind." Thus Spencer himself, at times, as these passages clearly show, sees that while great men, when considered philosophically, do little of what they appear to do, they must for practical purposes be dealt with as though they did all; though he nowhere recognises this distinction formally, or accords it a definite place in his general sociological system.[12]

The absurdity of confounding speculative sociology with practical is shown with equal clearness by Macaulay in the passage that was just now quoted from him. "The inequalities of the intellect," he says, "like the inequalities of the surface of the globe, bear so small a proportion to the mass" that the sociologist may neglect the one just as safely as the astronomer neglects the other. Now, this may be quite true if our interest in human events is that of social astronomers who are watching them from another planet. But because the inequalities of the earth are nothing to the astronomer, it does not follow that they are nothing to the engineer and the geographer. The Alps for the astronomer may be an infinitesimal and negligible excrescence; but they were not this to Hannibal or the makers of the Mont Cenis tunnel. What to the astronomer are all the dykes of Holland? But they are everything to the Dutch between a dead nation and a living one. And the same thing holds good of the inequalities of the human intellect. For the social astronomer they are nothing. For the practical man they are everything.

It is in the astonishing confusion between speculative and practical truth which characterised the evolutionary sociologists of the nineteenth century that the socialists of to-day are seeking for a new support to their system. And now let us consider the way in which they themselves have improved the occasion, and apply the moral which they have drawn from such a singularly deceptive source. The three points which they aim at emphasising are the smallness of the products which the able man can really claim as his own, the consequent diminution of his claims to any exceptional reward on account of them, and the fact that even the highest ability, however rare it may be, is very much commoner than it seems to be, and will, for this reason in addition to those just mentioned, be obtainable in the future at a very much reduced price.

Of these three points the last is the most definite. Let us take it first; and let us take it as stated, not by a professed socialist, but by an independent and highly educated thinker such as Mr. Kidd. Mr. Kidd's argument is, as we have seen already, that the comparative commonness of ability of the highest kind is shown by the fact that, of the greatest inventions and discoveries, a number have been notoriously made at almost the same time by a number of thinkers who have all worked in isolation. This argument would not be worth discussing if it were not used so constantly by a variety of serious writers. The fact on which it bases itself is no doubt true enough; but what is the utmost that it proves? That more men than one should reach at the same time the same discovery independently is precisely what we should be led to expect, when we consider what the character of scientific discovery is. The facts of nature which form its subject-matter are in themselves as independent of the men who discover them as an Alpine peak is of the men who attempt to climb it. They are, indeed, precisely analogous to such a peak which all discoverers are attempting to scale at once; and the fact that three men make at once the same discovery does no more to show that it could have been made by the majority of their fellow-workers, and that it was in reality made not by themselves but by their generation, than the fact that three men of exceptional nerve and endurance meet at last on some previously virgin summit proves the feat to have been accomplished less by these men themselves than by the mass of tourists who thronged the hotel below and whose climbing exploits were limited to an ascent by the Rigi Railway.

Other writers, however, try to reach Mr. Kidd's conclusion by a somewhat different route. Whether the great man is or is not a more common phenomenon than he seems to be, they maintain that his conquests in the realms of invention and discovery, when once made, really "become common property," of which all men could take advantage if it were not for artificial monopolies. All men, therefore, though not equal as discoverers, are practically equalised by whatever the discoverers accomplish. Now, of the simpler inventions and discoveries, such as that of fire for example, this is perfectly true; but it is true of these only. As inventions and discoveries grow more and more complex, they no more become common property, as soon as certain men have made them, than encyclop鎰ic knowledge becomes the property of every one who buys or happens to inherit an edition of the _Encyclop鎰ia Britannica_. It is perfectly true that the discovery of each new portion of knowledge enables men to acquire it who might never have acquired it otherwise; but as the acquisition of the details of knowledge becomes facilitated, the number of details to be acquired increases at the same time; and the increased ease of acquiring each is accompanied by an increased difficulty in assimilating even those which are connected most closely with each other. We may safely say that a knowledge of the simple rules of arithmetic is common to all the members of the English University of Cambridge; but out of some thousands of students only a few become great mathematicians. And the same thing holds good of scientific knowledge in general, and especially of such knowledge as applied to the purposes of practical industry. Knowledge and inventions, once made, are like a river which flows by everybody; but the water of the river becomes the property of individuals only in proportion to the quantity of it which their brains can, as it were, dip up; and the knowledge dipped up by the small brains is no more equal to that dipped up by the large than a tumbler of water is made equal to a hogshead by the fact that both vessels have been filled from the same stream.

Let us now pass on to the argument which, differing essentially from the preceding in that it does not aim at proving that the great men are commoner than they seem to be, or their knowledge more diffused, insists that of what the great men seem to do very little is really their own--or that, as Mr. Bellamy puts it, in words which we have already quoted, "nine hundred and ninety-nine parts out of a thousand of their produce is really the result of their social inheritance and environment." Here, again, we have a statement, which from one point of view is true. It is merely a specialised expression of the far more general doctrine that the whole process of the universe, man included, is one, and that all individual causes are only partial and proximate. No man at any period could do the precise things that he does if the country in which he lives had had a different past or present, any more than he could do anything if it were not for his own previous life, for the fact that he had been born, that his mind and body had matured, and that he had acquired, as he went along, such and such knowledge and experience. How could a man do anything unless he had some environment? Unless he had some past, how could he exist at all? Mr. Bellamy and his friends, when considering matters in this light, are not too extreme in their conclusions. On the contrary, they are too modest. For men, if they were really isolated from their social inheritance and environment, could not only do but little; they could do absolutely nothing. The admission, therefore, that for practical purposes they must be held to do something at all events, is an admission wrung from our philosophers by the exigencies of common-sense. As such, then, let us accept it; and what will our conclusion be? It will be this: that whatever it may be which the ordinary man produces, and in whatever sense he produces it, the great man, in the same sense, produces a great deal more. The difference between them in efficiency will be no more lessened by the fact that both are standing on the pedestal of a common past, than the difference in stature will be lessened between a dwarf and a giant because they are both standing on the top of a New York skyscraper, or because they have both been nourished on the same species of food.

But the practical absurdity of the whole set of arguments urged in a contrary sense by Herbert Spencer, Mr. Kidd, and the speculative sociologists generally, is brought to its climax by those modern exponents of socialism who attempt to invest them with a moral as well as an industrial significance. Thus Mr. Webb, who himself frankly recognises that the monopolists of business ability are industrially more efficient than the great mass of their fellows, and that man for man they produce incomparably more wealth, endeavours, by means of the arguments which we have been just considering, to show that though they produce it they have no moral right to keep it. The proposal, he says, that, though men are vastly unequal in productivity, they should all of them be awarded an equal share of the product--that if one man produces only one shilling, while another man produces ninety-nine, the resulting hundred should be halved and each of the men take fifty--this proposal "has," he says, "an abstract justification, as the special energy and ability with which some persons are born is an unearned increment due to the effect of the struggle for existence upon their ancestors, and consequently, having been produced by society, is as much due to society as the unearned increment of rent."

Now, if this argument has any practical meaning at all, it can only mean that the men who have been born with such special powers will, as soon as they recognise what the origin of these powers is, realise that they have, as individuals, no special claims on the results of them, and will consequently become more willing than they are at the present time to continue to produce the results, though they will not be allowed to keep them. We will not insist, as we might do, on the curious want of knowledge of human nature which the argument thus put forward by Mr. Webb and other socialists betrays. It will be enough to point out that, if it applies to the monopolists of business ability, it applies with equal force to all other sorts of men whatever. If it is to society as a whole that the able man owes his energy, his talents, and the products of them, it is to society as a whole that the idle man owes his idleness, the stupid man his stupidity, and the dishonest man his dishonesty; and if the able man, who produces an exceptional amount of wealth, can with justice claim no more than the average man who produces little, the man who is so idle that he shirks producing anything may with equal justice claim as much wealth as either. His constitutional fault, and his constitutional disinclination to mend it, are both of them due to society, and society, not he, must suffer.

If we attempted to organise a community in accordance with such a conclusion as this, we should be getting rid of all connection between conduct and the natural results of it, and divorcing action from motive altogether. Such is the conclusion to which Mr. Webb's argument would lead us; and the absurdity of the argument, as applied by him to moral claims and merits, though more self-evident, is not any more complete than the absurdity of similar arguments as applied to the individual generally in respect of his productive powers, and the amount of produce produced by them. The whole conception, in short, of the individual as merged in the aggregate has no relation to practical life whatever. For the practical man the individual is always a unit; and it is only as a unit that it is possible practically to deal with him. We may change him in some respects by changing his general conditions, as we hope to do by legislation which aims at the diminution of drunkenness; but a change in general conditions, if it diminished drunkenness generally, would do so only because it affected at the same time the isolated minds and organisms of a number of individual drunkards.

And to do Mr. Webb and his brother socialists justice, they unconsciously admit all this themselves; for, as soon as they set themselves to discuss the motives of the able man in detail, they altogether abandon the irrelevancies of speculative sociology with which they manage at other times to bemuse themselves. That such is the case we shall see in the following chapter. I will, however, anticipate what we shall see there by mentioning that among the motives which are in the socialistic future to replace, among able men, the desire of economic gain, one of the chief is to be the desire of moral approbation. Unless a man's actions, whether industrial or moral, are to be treated as his own, instead of being attributed to his conditions, he would have as little right to the praise which it is proposed to give him as he would have to the dollars which it is proposed to take away.

FOOTNOTES:

[12] I first made this criticism of Spencer in my work Aristocracy and Evolution. On that occasion Mr. Spencer wrote to me, complaining with much vehemence that I had misrepresented him; and he repeated the substance of his letter in a subsequent published essay. My criticism dealt, and could have dealt only, not with what he meant, but what he said; and certainly in his language--and, as I think, in his own mind--there was a constant confusion between the two truths in question. Apart, however, from what he considered to be my own misrepresentation of himself, he declared that he entirely agreed with me; and that "great men" must, for practical purposes, be regarded as the true causes of such changes as they initiate.

CHAPTER IX

THE ULTIMATE DIFFICULTY, CONTINUED. ABILITY AND INDIVIDUAL MOTIVE

The fact that the speculative arguments which we have just now been discussing are not only irrelevant to the problem of the able man and his motives, but are tacitly abandoned as being so by the very men who have urged them, when they come to deal specifically with that problem themselves, may suggest to some readers that so long a discussion of them was superfluous. But though the socialists abandon them at the very moment when, if ever, they ought to be susceptible of some definite application, they abandon them quite unconsciously, and still continue to attach to them some solemn importance. Such being the case, then, the more futile these arguments are the stronger is the light thrown by them on the peculiar intellectual weakness which distinguishes even the most capable of those who think it worth their while to employ them. For this reason, therefore, if for no other, our examination of them will have proved useful, for it will have prepared us to encounter a weakness of precisely the same kind in the reasonings of the socialists when they deal with motive directly.

Let us once more state this direct problem of motive, as with perfect accuracy, stated by the socialists themselves. Under existing conditions the monopolists of business ability are mainly induced to add to the national store of wealth by the prospect, whose fulfilment existing conditions make possible, of retaining shares of it as their own which are proportionate to the amounts produced by them. The question is, therefore, whether, if this prospect is taken away from them, socialism could provide another which men of this special type would find equally stimulating. Is human nature in general, and the nature of the monopolists in particular, sufficiently adaptable to admit of such a change as this? The socialists answer that it is, and in making such an assertion they declare that they have all the facts of scientific sociology at the back of them. The unscientific thing is, they say, to assume the contrary; and here, they proceed, we have the fundamental error which renders most of the conclusions of the ordinary economists valueless. Economic science, in its generally accepted form, bases all its reasonings on the behaviour of the so-called "economic man"--that is to say, a being from whom those who reason about him exclude all operative desires except that of economic gain. But such a being, say the socialists, is a mere abstraction. He has no counterpart among living, loving, idealising, aspiring men. Real men are susceptible of the desire of gain, no doubt; but this provides them only with one motive out of many; and there are others which, as experience amply shows us, are, when they are given unimpeded play, far stronger. I do not know whether socialists have ever used the following parallel; but if they have not it expresses their position better than they have expressed it themselves. They argue virtually that, in respect of the desire for exceptional gain, able men are comparable to victims of the desire for alcohol. If alcohol is obtainable, such men will insist on obtaining it. They will constantly fix their thoughts on it; no other fluid will satisfy them. But if it is placed altogether beyond their reach, they will be compelled by the force of circumstances to drink lemonade, tea, or even plain water instead. In time they will come to drink them with the same avidity; and their health and their powers of enjoyment will be indefinitely improved in consequence. In the same way, it is argued, the monopolists of business ability, though, so long as it is possible for them to appropriate a considerable share of their products, they will insist on getting this share, and will not exert themselves otherwise, need only be placed under conditions which will render such gain impossible, and at once they will find out that there exist other inducements which will prove before long to be no less efficacious.

Such is the general argument of the modern school of socialists; but they do not leave it in this indeterminate form. They have, to their own satisfaction, worked it out in detail, and claim that they are able to demonstrate from the actual facts of human nature precisely what the character of the new inducements will be.

It may be looked upon as evidence of the methodical and quasi-scientific accuracy with which modern socialists have set themselves to discuss this question of motive that the thought of all of them has moved along the same lines, and that what all of them fix upon as a substitute for the desire of exceptional pecuniary gain is one or other, or all, of a few motives actually in operation, and notoriously effective in certain spheres of activity.

These motives practically resolve themselves into four, which have been classified as follows by Mr. Webb or one of his coadjutors:

"The mere pleasure of excelling," or the joy of the most powerful in exercising their powers to the utmost.

"The joy in creative work," such as that which the artist feels in producing a great work of art.

The satisfaction which ministering to others "brings to the instincts of benevolence," such as that which is felt by those who give themselves to the sick and helpless.

And, lastly, the desire for approval, or the homage which is called "honour," the efficiency of which is shown by the conduct of the soldier--often a man of very ordinary education and character--who will risk death in order that he may be decorated with some intrinsically worthless medal, which merely proclaims his valour or his unselfish devotion to his country.

Now, that the motives here in question are motives of extraordinary power, all history shows us. The most impressive things accomplished by human nature have been due to them. But let us consider what these things are. The first motive--namely, that supplied by the mere "pleasure in excelling"--we need hardly consider by itself, for, in so far as socialists can look upon its objects as legitimate, it is included in the struggle for approbation or honour. We will merely remark that the emphasis which the socialists lay on it is not very consonant with the principles of those persons who propose to abolish competition as the root of all social evils; and we will content ourselves with examining in detail the three other motives only, and the scope of their efficiency, as actual experience reveals it to us.

We shall find that the activities which these three motives stimulate are confined, so far as experience is able to teach us anything, to the following well-marked kinds, which have been already indicated: those of the artist, of the speculative thinker, of the religious and philanthropic enthusiast, and, lastly, those of the soldier. This list, if understood in its full sense, is exhaustive.

Such being the case, then, the argument of the socialists is as follows: Because a Fra Angelico will paint a Christ or a Virgin, because a Kant will immolate all his years to philosophy, because a monk and a sister of mercy will devote themselves to the victims of pestilence, because a soldier in action will eagerly face death--all without hope of any exceptional pecuniary reward--the monopolists of business ability, if only such rewards are made impossible for them, will at once become amenable to the motives of the soldier, the artist, the philosopher, the inspired philanthropist, and the saint. This is the assertion of the socialists when reduced to a precise form; and what we have to do is to inquire whether this assertion is true. Does human nature, as history, as psychology, and as physiology reveal it to us, give us any grounds, in fact, for taking such an assertion seriously? Any one who has studied human conduct historically, who has observed it in the life around him, and examined scientifically the diversities of temperament and motive that go with diversities of capacity, will dismiss such an assertion as at once groundless and ludicrous.

Let us, to go into detail, take the case of the artist. What reason is there to suppose that the impassioned emotion which stimulates the adoring monk to lavish all his genius on an altar-piece will stimulate another man to devise, and to organise the production of, some new kind of liquid enamel for the decoration of cheap furniture?[13] Or let us turn to an impulse closely allied to the artistic--namely, the desire for speculative truth, as manifested in the lives of scientific and philosophic thinkers. These men--such as Kant and Hegel, for example--have been proverbially, and often ludicrously, indifferent to the material details of their existence. Who can suppose that the disinterested passion for truth, which had the effect of making these men forget their dinners, will stimulate others to devote themselves to the improvement of stoves and saucepans?

Yet again, let us consider the area of the industrial influence of the motives originating in religious fervour or benevolence. The most important illustration of this is to be found in the monastic orders. The monastic orders constructed great buildings; they successfully practised agriculture and other industrial arts: and those of them who were faithful to their vows aimed at no personal luxuries. On the contrary, their superfluous possessions were applied by them to the relief of indigence. But this industrial asceticism was made possible only by its association with another asceticism--the renunciation of women, the private home, the family. Even so, in the days when Christian piety was at its highest, those who were capable of responding to the industrial motives of the cloister formed but a fraction of the general population of Christendom, while even among them these motives constantly ceased to operate; and, as St. Francis declared with regard to his own disciples, the desire for personal gain continually insisted on reasserting itself. What ground have we here for supposing that motives, whose action hitherto has always been strictly limited to passionate and seclusive idealists turning their backs on the world, will ever become general among the monopolists of that business ability, the object of whom is to fill the world with increasing comforts and luxuries. One might as well argue that, because the monastic orders were celibate, and formed at one time a very numerous body, all men will probably soon turn celibate also, and yet at the same time continue to reproduce their species.

But the scientific quality of the psychological reasoning of the socialists is best illustrated by their treatment of another class of facts--that on which they themselves unanimously lay the greatest stress--namely, the heroisms of the soldier, and other men of a kindred type. The soldier, they say, is not only willing but eager to perform duties of the most painful and dangerous kind, without any thought of receiving any higher pay than his fellows. If, then, human nature is such, they continue, that we can get from it on these terms work such as that of the soldier's, which is work in its most terrifying form, it stands to reason that we can, on the same terms, get out of it work of a much easier kind, such as that of exceptional business ability applied to the safe and peaceful direction of labour. Nor is this argument urged by socialists only. Other thinkers who, though resembling them somewhat in sentiment, are wholly opposed to socialism as a formal creed, have likewise pitched upon the soldier's conduct in war as a signal illustration of the potentialities of human nature in peace. Thus Ruskin says that his whole scheme of political economy is based on the moral assimilation of industrial action to military. "Soldiers of the ploughshare," he exclaims in one of his works, "as well as soldiers of the sword! All my political economy is comprehended in that phrase." So, too, Mr. Frederic Harrison, the English prophet of Positivism, following out the same train of thought, has declared that the soldier's readiness to die in battle for his country is a realised example of a readiness, always latent in men, to spend themselves and be spent in the service of humanity generally. Again in the same sense, another writer observes, "The soldier's subsistence is certain. It does not depend on his exertions. At once he becomes susceptible to appeals to his patriotism, and he will value a bit of bronze, which is the reward of valour, far more than a hundred times its weight in gold"--a passage to which one of Mr. Sidney Webb's collaborators refers with special delight, exclaiming, "Let those take notice of this last fact who fancy we must wait till men are angels before socialism is practical."

Now, the arguments thus drawn from the facts of military activity throw a special light on the methods and mental condition of those who so solemnly urge them; for the error by which these arguments are vitiated is of a peculiarly glaring kind. It consists of a failure to perceive that military activity is, in many respects, a thing altogether apart, and depends on psychological and physiological conditions which have no analogies in the domain of ordinary economic effort.

That such must necessarily be the case can be very easily seen by following out the train of reasoning suggested by Mr. Frederic Harrison. Mr. Harrison correctly assumes that no man, in ordinary life, will run the risk of being killed or mutilated except for the sake of some object the achievement of which is profoundly desired by him. If a man, for instance, puts his hand into the fire in order to pick out something that has dropped among the burning coals, we naturally assume that this something is of the utmost value and importance to him. We measure the value which a man places on the object by the desperate character of the means which he will take to gain it; and Mr. Harrison jumps to the conclusion that what holds good in ordinary life will hold equally good on the field of battle also. Hence he argues--for this is his special point--that the willingness of the soldier to die fighting on behalf of his country shows how individuals of no unusual kind value their country's welfare more than their own lives, and how readily, such being the case, devotion to a particular country may be enlarged into a religious devotion to Humanity taken as a whole. Now, there are occasions, no doubt, in which, a country being in desperate straits, the soldier's valour is heightened by devotion to the cause he fights for; but that ideal devotion like this affords no sufficient explanation of the peculiar character of military activity generally; and that there must be some deeper and more general cause at the back of it, is shown by the fact that some of the most reckless soldiers known to us have been mercenaries who would fight as willingly for one country as for another. And this deeper and more general cause, when we look for it, is sufficiently obvious. It consists of the fact that, owing to the millions of years of struggle to which was due, in the first place, the evolution of man as a species, and, in the second place, the races of men in their existing stages of civilisation, the fighting instinct is, in the strongest of these races, inherent after a fashion in which the industrial instincts are not; and will always prompt numbers to do, for the smallest wage or none, what they could hardly, in its absence, be induced to do for the highest. This instinct, no doubt, is more controlled than formerly, and is not so often roused; but it is still there. It is ready to quicken at the mere sound of military music; and the sight of regiments marching stirs the most apathetic crowd. High-spirited boys will, for the mere pleasure of fighting, run the risk of having their noses broken, while they will wince at getting up in the cold for the sake of learning their lessons, and would certainly rebel against being set to work as wage-earners at a task which involved so much as a daily pricking of their fingers.

Here we have the reason, embodied in the very organism of the human being, why military activity is something essentially distinct from industrial, and why any inference drawn from the one to the other is valueless. And to this primary fact it is necessary to add another. Not only is the fighting instinct an exceptional phenomenon in man, but the circumstances which call it into being are in these days exceptional also. Socialists frequently, when referring to the soldier's conduct, refer also to conduct of a closely allied kind, such as that of the members of fire-brigades and the crews of life-boats, and repeat their previous question of why, since men like these will, without demanding any exceptional reward, make such exceptional efforts to save the lives of others, the monopolists of business ability may not be reasonably expected to forgo all exceptional claims on their own exceptional products, and distribute among all the superfluous wealth produced by them just as freely as the fireman climbs his ladder, or as life-belts are distributed by the boatmen in their work of rescue. And if human life were nothing but a chronic conflagration or shipwreck, in which all alike were fighting for bare existence, all alike being menaced by some terrible and instant death, this argument of the socialists might doubtless have some truth in it. The men of exceptional ability, by a variety of ingenious devices, might seek to save others no less assiduously than themselves, without expecting anything like exceptional wealth as a reward; for there would, in a case like this, be no question of wealth for anybody. But as soon as the stress of such a situation was relaxed, and the abilities of the ablest, liberated from the task of contending with death, were left free to devote themselves to the superfluous decoration of life, the artificial tension of the moral motives would be relaxed. The swimmer who had plunged into the sea to save a woman from drowning would not take a second plunge to rescue her silk petticoat. The socialists, in short, when dealing with military and other cognate heroisms, ignore both of the causes which alone make such heroisms possible. They ignore the fact that the internal motive is essentially isolated and exceptional. They ignore the further fact that the circumstances which alone give this motive play are essentially exceptional also, and could never be reproduced in social life at large, except at the cost of making all human life intolerable.

I have called special attention to this particular socialistic argument, partly because socialists, and other sentimental thinkers, like Ruskin, attach such extreme importance to it; but mainly because it affords us an exceptionally striking illustration of the manner in which they are accustomed to reason about matters with regard to which they ostentatiously profess themselves to be the pioneers of accurate science. One of the principal grounds--to repeat what has been said already--on which they attack what they call the Economics of Capitalism, is that it deals exclusively with the actions of "the economic man," or the man whose one motive is the appropriation of wealth. Such a man, they say, is an abstraction. He does not exist in reality; and if economics is to have any scientific value it must deal with man as a whole, in all his living complexity. As applied to the orthodox economists this criticism has an element of truth in it; but when the socialists attempt to act on their own loudly boasted principles, and deal with human nature as a whole instead of only one of its elements, they do nothing but travesty the error which they set out with denouncing. The one-motived economic man who cares only for personal gain is, no doubt, an abstraction, like the lines and points of Euclid. Still the motive ascribed to him is one which has a real existence and produces real effects. It has been defined with accuracy; and by studying its effects in isolation we reach many true conclusions. But the other motives, with which socialists declare that we must supplement this, are treated by them in a manner so crude, so childish, so incomplete, so deficient in the mere rudiments of scientific analysis, that they do not correspond to anything. Instead of forming any true addition to the data of economic science, they are like images belonging to the dream of a maudlin school-girl. They have only the effect of obscuring, not completing, the facts to which the orthodox economists too closely confined themselves, but which, though incomplete, are so far as they go actual.

Now, however, without getting out of touch with the socialists, let us return to firmer ground, and having seen the futility of their attempts to indicate any motive calculated to operate on the monopolists of business ability, other than that supplied under the existing system by the prospect of possessing wealth proportionate to the amount produced by them, let us consider this motive in itself, as history and observation reveal it to us.

And here in the presence of facts which no one seeks to deny, we shall find that the socialists themselves are among our most interesting witnesses, affording in what they assert a solitary and signal exception to that looseness of thought and observation which is otherwise their distinguishing characteristic. The motive here in question as ascribed to the exceptional wealth-producer, the director, the man of business ability--the motive which in his case the socialists propose to supersede, but which is at present in possession of the field--commonly receives from them the vituperative name of "greed." What they mean by greed is simply the desire of the great wealth-producer to retain for himself a share of wealth, not necessarily equal, but proportionate, to the amount produced by him. And what have the socialists got to tell us about greed, when they turn from their plans for superseding it in the socialistic future to consider its operations in the actual past and present?

They tell us a great deal. For what is, and always has been, their stock moral indictment against the typical men of ability, the pioneers of commerce, the capitalistic directors of labour, the introducers of new inventions, the amplifiers of the world's wealth? Their chief indictment against such men has been this--that their exceptional ability, instead of being roused into action solely by the pleasure of benefiting their fellow-men, has been utterly dead and irresponsive to every stimulus but one; and that this has been personal greed, and personal greed alone. Its influence, they say, is as old as civilisation itself, and was as operative in the days when the prows of the Tyrian traders first ploughed their way beyond the pillars of Hercules, as it is to-day under the smoke-clouds of Manchester, of Pittsburg, and Chicago. Karl Marx for example, in a very interesting passage written in England about the time of the abolition of the Corn-laws, declared that the radical manufacturers, who professed to support that measure on the ground that it would secure cheap food for the people, were not moved in reality, and were not capable of being moved, by any desire but that of lowering the rate of wages, and thus increasing the surplus which they raked into their own pockets. In other words, the psychologists of socialism declare that, so far as the facts of human nature in the present and the past can teach us anything, the desire of exceptional wealth is just as inseparable from the temperament which, by some physiological law, accompanies the power of producing it, as "the joy in creation" is from the temperament of the great painter, or the love of a woman is from the lover's efforts to win her.

We thus see that those thinkers who, when they are dealing with an imaginary future, base all their hopes on the possibility of a complete elimination of a certain motive from a certain special class of persons, are the very men who are most vehement in declaring that in this special class of persons the motive in question is something so ingrained and inveterate that in no age or country has it ever been so much as modified.

Nor does the matter end here; for the amusing contradiction in which socialistic thought thus lauds itself, is emphasised by the fact that the socialists, when they turn from the few to the many, assume in the many, as an instinct of eternal justice, that precise desire for gain which, in the case of the few, they first denounce as a hideous and incurable disease, and then propose to cure as though it were the passing cough of a baby. For what is the bait with which, from its first beginnings till to-day, socialism has sought to secure the support of the general multitude? It is mainly, if not solely, the promise of increased personal gain, without any increased effort on the part of the happy recipients. With Marx and the earlier socialists, this promise took the form of declaring that every man has a sacred right to whatever he has himself produced, and that, all the wealth of the world being produced by manual labour, the labourers must never be satisfied until they have secured all of it. The more educated socialists of to-day, having gradually come to perceive that labour itself produces but a fraction of this wealth only, have had to alter the form of their promise, but they still adhere to its substance; and the altered form of the promise does but bring out more clearly the fact that they appeal to the desire of personal gain as the primary economic motive of the great majority of mankind. For, whereas the earlier socialists contented themselves with promising the labourer the whole of what he produced, and promising it on the ground that he had himself produced it, what the labourer is promised by the intellectual socialists of to-day is not only all that he has produced--which in most cases he gets already[14]--but a great deal more besides, which is admittedly produced by others.

We thus see that, according to these theorists, the kind of moral conversion which is to make socialism practicable is to be rigidly confined to one particular class; for, on the part of the majority, no change at all is required in order to make the socialistic evangel welcome. So far as they are concerned, the Old Adam is quite sufficient. None of us need much converting in order to welcome the prospect of an indefinite addition to our incomes, which will cost us nothing but the trouble of stretching out our hands to take it. Socialists often complain that, under the existing dispensation, there is one law for the rich and another law for the poor. They propose themselves to introduce a difference which goes still deeper, and to provide the few and the many, not only with two laws, but with two different natures, and two antithetic moralities. The morality of the many is to remain, as it always has been, comfortably based on the familiar desire for dollars. The morality of the few is to be based on some hitherto unknown contempt for them; and the class which the socialists fix upon as the subjects of this moral transformation, is precisely the class which they denounce as being, and as always having been, in respect of its devotion to dollars, the most notorious, and the most notoriously incorrigible.

That arguments such as these, culminating in an absurdity like this, and starting with the assumption that it is possible to animate a manufacturer's office with the spirit of soldiers facing an enemy's guns, should actually emanate from sane men would be unbelievable, if the arguments were not being repeated from day to day by men who, in some respects, are far from being incompetent reasoners. Indeed, many of them themselves would, it seems, be extremely doubtful with regard to the plasticity imputed by them to human nature, if it were not for a theory of society which is not peculiar to socialism. This is the theory that, in any community or nation in which each citizen is completely free to express his will by his vote, and realises the extent of the power which thus resides in him, the will of the majority has practically no limits to its efficiency, and will be able in the future to bring about moral changes, which are at present, perhaps, beyond the limits of possibility, but are only so because the means of effecting them have never yet been fully utilised. This theory of democracy we will consider in the following chapter.

FOOTNOTES:

[13] Mr. G. Wilshire, in criticising this argument as stated in one of my American addresses, declares that there would be nothing in socialism to prevent any great artist (such as a singer) from making an even larger fortune than he or she does now. But though a Melba, under the existing system, demands a large price for her services, under socialism all would be changed. Though she could get it, she would no longer want it. She would then want no reward but the mere joy of using her voice. And he infers that this change which would take place in the bosoms of great singers would repeat itself under the breast-pocket of every leader and organiser of commercial enterprise. It would be hard to find a better illustration of the purely fanciful reasoning commented on in the text.

[14] The question of how much labour, as such, produces in modern societies is discussed in a later chapter.

CHAPTER X

INDIVIDUAL MOTIVE AND DEMOCRACY

The ascription of imaginary powers to the so-called "sovereign" democracy, which are really beyond the reach of any kind of government whatsoever, is, as I have said, a fallacy by no means peculiar to Socialists. Socialists merely push it to its full logical consequences; and I will begin with illustrating it by the arguments of a recent writer who, professedly as a social conservative, has dealt in detail with this precise question of the motives of the exceptional wealth-producer, which has just now been engaging us. I refer to the author of an essay in The North American Review, who hides his personality under the cryptic initial "X," but who is said to be one of the most cultivated and best-known thinkers now living in the United States.

The subject of his essay is the growth, almost peculiar to that country, not of large, but of those colossal fortunes, which have certainly had no parallel in the past history of the world. The position of "X" is that the growth of such fortunes is deplorable, partly because they are possible instruments of judicial and political corruption, and partly because they excite antagonism against private wealth in general by exhibiting it to the gaze of the multitude in such monstrous and grotesque proportions. In any case, says "X," "it is to the true interest of the multimillionaires themselves to join those who are free from envy in trying to remove the rapidly growing dissatisfaction with their continued possession of these vast sums of money."

Now, though "X" hints that some of the fortunes in question may be open to further reprehension, on the ground that they have been acquired dishonestly, he by no means maintains that this opprobrium attaches itself to the great majority of them. On the contrary, he admits that the typical huge fortunes of America are based on the productive activities of the remarkable men who have amassed them. The talents of such men, he says, are essential to the prosperity of the country, and it is necessary to stimulate such men to develop their talents to the utmost by allowing them to derive for themselves some special reward for their use of them; but he contends that the rewards which they are at present permitted to appropriate are needlessly and dangerously excessive, and ought therefore to be limited. But limited by what means? It is his answer to this question that here alone concerns us.

The means, he says, by which these rewards may be limited are ready to hand, and can be applied with the utmost ease. They are provided by the democratic Constitution of the United States of America. "No one can doubt, for example," he goes on to observe, "that, if the majority of the voters of the State of New York chose to elect a governor of their own way of thinking, they could readily enact a progressive taxation of incomes which would limit every citizen of New York State to such income as the majority of voters considers sufficient for him. And it would be particularly easy," adds the writer, "to alienate the property of every man at death, for it is only necessary to repeal the statutes now authorising the descent of such property to the heirs and legatees of the decedent." Here, then, according to "X," is an obvious way out of the difficulty, the feasibility of which no one can doubt. A certain minority of the citizens render services essential to the majority; but these advantages are accompanied by a corresponding drawback. The majority, by the simple use of their sovereign power as legislators, can retain the former and get rid of the latter. The remedy is in their own hands.

It would be difficult to imagine an illustration more vivid than this of the error to which I am now referring--the common error of ascribing to majorities in democratic communities powers which they do not possess, and which, as I said before, no kind of government possesses, whether it be that of a democracy or of an autocrat. That a majority of the voters in any democratic country can enact any laws they please at any given moment which happen to be in accordance with what "X" calls their then "way of thinking," and perhaps enforce them for a moment, is no doubt perfectly true. But life is not made up of isolated moments or periods. It is a continuous process, in which each moment is affected by the moments that have gone before, and by the prospective character of the moments that are to come after. If it were not for this fact, the majority of the voters of New York State, "by electing a governor of their own way of thinking," might not only put a limit to the income which any citizen might possess. It might do a great deal more besides. It might enact a law which limited the amount which any citizen might eat. It might limit everybody to two ounces a day. Besides enacting that no father should bequeath his wealth to his children, it might enact just as readily that no father should have the custody of his children. It might enact, in obedience to the persuasions of some plausible quack, that no one should take any medicines but a single all-curing pill. There is nothing in the principles so solemnly laid down by "X" which would render any of these enactments more impossible than those which he himself contemplates. But if such enactments were made by the so-called all-powerful majority, through a governor of their own way of thinking, what would be the result? If a law forbade the citizens to eat enough to keep themselves alive, it might perhaps be obeyed throughout Monday, but it would be broken by Tuesday morning. A law which deprived fathers of the care of their own children might just as well be a law which decreed that no children should be born. A law which decreed that no remedy but the same quack pill should be applied to any disease, whether cholera, appendicitis, or small-pox, would be either disregarded from the beginning, or would soon be repealed by a pestilence. In short, if any one of these ridiculous laws were enacted, the very voters who voted for it would disregard it as soon as they realised its consequences; and the work which they did as legislators they would tear to pieces as men. In other words, if we mean, by legislation, legislation which can be permanently obeyed, the legislative sovereignty of democracies, which is so commonly spoken of as supreme, is limited in every direction by another power greater than itself; and this is the double power of nature and of human nature. Just as all laws relating to the food which men are to eat, and the drugs by which their maladies are to be cured, must depend on the natural qualities of such and such physical substances, so do the constitution and propensities of the concrete human character limit legislation generally, and confine it within certain channels.

This is what "X" and similar thinkers forget; and the nature of their error is very pertinently illustrated by an observation of the English jurist, Lord Coleridge, to which "X" solemnly refers, as corroborating him in his own wisdom. "The same power," says Lord Coleridge, "which prescribes rules for the possession of property can of course alter them"; this power being the legislative body of whatever country may be in question. It is easy to see the manner in which Lord Coleridge reasons. Because, in any country, the formulation and enforcement of laws have the will of the governing body as the proximate cause which determines them, it seems to Lord Coleridge that, in this contemporary will, the laws thus formulated and enforced have their ultimate cause also. For example, according to him, the entire institution of property in the State of New York is virtually a fresh creation of the voters from year to year, and has nothing else behind it. But, in reality, all this business of formulation and enforcement is a secondary process, not a primary process at all. Lord Coleridge is simply inverting the actual order of things. Half the existing "rules prescribed as to the possession of property" have, for their ultimate object, the protection of family life, the privacy of the private home, and the provision made by parents for their children. But family life is not primarily the creation of prescribed rules. It is the creation of instincts and affections which have developed themselves in the course of ages. Instead of the law creating family life, it is family life which has gradually called into being--which has created and dictated--the rules and sanctions protecting it. The same is the case with bequest, marriage, and so forth. The conduct of civilised men is bound to conform to laws, but the laws must first conform to general human practice. They merely give precision to conduct which has a deeper origin than legislation. Laws, in fact, may be compared to soldiers' uniforms. These, within certain limits, may be varied indefinitely by a war-office; but they all must be such as will adapt themselves to the human body and its movements. The will of a government may prescribe that the trousers shall be tight or loose, that they shall be black or brown or bright green or vermilion. But no government can prescribe that they shall be only three inches round the waist, or that the soldier's sleeves shall start, not from the shoulders, but from the pockets of the coat-tails. The human body is here a legislator which is supreme over all governments; and just the same thing is true with regard to the human character.

Now, the curious thing with regard to "X" is that he is all along assuming this fundamental fact himself; though he utterly fails to put two and two together, and see how this fact conflicts with the omnipotence which he ascribes to legislation. Let us go back to the assertion, which embodies his whole practical argument, that the majority of the voters in New York State could, without interfering with the activity of any one of its citizens, limit incomes in any manner they pleased, and alienate with even greater ease the property of every man at his death; and let us see what he hastens to say as the sequel to this oracular utterance.

These powers of the sovereign majority, which he is apparently so anxious to invoke, would, he says, be practically much less formidable in their action than timid persons might anticipate. And why should they be less formidable? "Because," says "X," "although each man, by reason of his manhood alone, has an equal voice with every other man in making the laws governing their common country, and regulating the distribution of the common property ... yet immense and incalculable differences exist in men's natural capacities for rendering honest service to society. Encouragement should, therefore, be given to every man to use all the gifts which he possesses to the fullest extent possible; and, accordingly, reasonable accumulations and the descent of these should be respected." They should, he says, be respected. Yes--but for what reason? Because they encourage exceptional men, whose services are essential to society, to develop and use their capacities to "the fullest extent possible"; and this is merely another way of saying that, without the motive provided by the possibility of accumulation and bequest, the exceptional faculties would not be developed or used at all. Moreover, the amounts which may be accumulated and bequeathed, although they will be strictly limited, must, "X" says, be considerable. He suggests that incomes should be allowed up to ?,000, and bequeathable property up to ?00,000. And here we come to a question which is still more pertinent than the preceding. Why must the permissible amounts of income and of bequeathable property be of proportions such as those which he contemplates? Why does he not take his bill and write down quickly ?00 of income instead of ?,000, and limit bequeathable property to ?,000 instead of ?00,000? Because he evidently recognises that the men whose possible services to society are "immensely and incalculably greater" than those of the majority of their fellow citizens would not be tempted by a reward which, reduced to its smallest proportions, would not be very largely in excess of what was attainable by more ordinary exertions. In his formal statement of his case, he says that the amount of the reward would be entirely determined by what ought to be sufficient for the purpose in the estimation of the voting majority; and he mentions the sums in question as those on which they would probably fix. And it is, of course, quite imaginable that the majority, in making either these or any other estimates, might be right. But what "X" fails altogether to see is that, if the majority of the citizens were right, such sums would not be sufficient because the majority of citizens happened to think that they ought to be. They would be sufficient because they were felt to be sufficient by the minority who were invited to earn them, at whose feelings the majority would have made a shrewd or a lucky guess. A thousand men with fishing-rods might meet in an inn parlour and vote that such and such flies were sufficient to attract trout. But it lies with the trout to determine whether or no he will rise to them. It is a question, not of what the fishermen think, but of what the trout thinks; and the fishermen's thoughts are effective only when they coincide with the trout's.

So long, then, as society desires to get the best work out of its citizens, and so long as some men are, in the words of "X," "immensely and incalculably" more efficient than the great mass of their fellows, and so long as their efficiency requires, as "X" admits that it does, some exceptional reward to induce these men to develop it, these men themselves, in virtue of their inherent characters, must primarily determine what the reward shall be; and not all the majorities in the world, however unanimous, could make a reward sufficient if the particular minority in question did not feel it to be so. The majority might, by making a sufficient reward unattainable, easily prevent the services from being rendered at all; but, unless they are to forgo the services, the majority can only obtain them on terms which will, in the last resort, depend on the men who are to render them.

Now, in what I have been urging thus far--which practically comes to this, that the sovereignty popularly ascribed to democratic majorities is an illusion--not socialists only, but other advocates of popular government also, will alike be against me, as the promulgator of some blasphemous paradox. It will be easy, however, to show them that their objections are quite mistaken, and that the exceptional powers of dictation which have just been ascribed to a minority are so far from being inconsistent with the real powers of the majority that the latter, when properly understood, are seen to be their complement and their counterpart. For, though socialists and thinkers like "X" ascribe to majorities powers which they do not possess, we shall find that majorities do actually possess others, in some ways very much greater, of which such thinkers have thus far taken no cognisance at all. I have said that minorities can dictate their own terms to majorities which desire to secure their services, the reason being that the former are alone competent to determine what treatment will supply them with a motive to exert themselves. What holds good of minorities as opposed to majorities holds good in essentials, though in a somewhat different form, of majorities as opposed to such minorities.

Let us turn again to a matter to which I have referred already--namely, the family life of the citizens of any race or nation. This results from propensities in a vast number of human beings which, although they are similar, are in each case independent. These propensities give rise to legislation, the object of which is to prescribe rules by which their satisfaction may be made secure; but the propensities are so far from originating in legislation that no legislation which seriously interfered with them would be tolerated. Socialists themselves have continually admitted this very thing. The Italian socialist, Giovanni Rossi, for instance, who attempted about fifteen years ago to found a socialistic colony in Brazil--an attempt which completely failed--attributed its failure largely to this particular cause--namely, the impossibility of inducing the colonists to conform to any rules of the community by which family life was interfered with. Here we have an example of democracy in its genuine form, rendering powerless what affected to be democratic legislation. We have the cumulative power of similar human characters compelling legislation to limit itself to what these characters spontaneously demand. And now let us go a step--a very short step--further. The family propensities in question show their dictatorial power, not only in the limitations which they impose on positive laws, but also in the character which they impose on the material surroundings of existence, especially in the material structure of the dwellings of all classes except the lowest. All are constructed with a view to keeping the family group united, and each family group separate from all others. Further, if the natural family propensities thus affect the structure of the dwelling, other propensities, more various in detail, but in each case equally spontaneous, determine what commodities shall be put into it.

And this fact brings us back to our own more immediate subject--namely, the power of the few and of the many in the sphere of economic production. The man of exceptional industrial capacity becomes rich in the modern world by producing goods, or by rendering services, which others consume or profit by, and for which they render him a return. But, in order that they may take, and render him this return for what he offers them, the goods and the services must be such that the many desire to have them. All the highest productive ability that has ever been devoted to the business of cheapening and multiplying commodities, or rendering social services, would be absolutely futile unless these commodities and services satisfied tastes or wants existing in various sections of the community. The eliciting of such wants or tastes depends very often, and in progressive communities usually, on a previous supply of the commodities or services that minister to them--as we see, for example, in the case of tobacco, of the telegraph, and of the bicycle; but, when once the demands have been elicited, they are essentially democratic in their nature. Each customer is like a voter who practically gives his vote for the kind of goods which he desires to have supplied to him. He gives his vote under no compulsion. He is under the manipulation of no party or wire-puller; and the men by whose ability the goods are cheapened and multiplied are bound to determine their character by the number of votes cast for them.[15]

Thus, while--so long as the productivity of labour is intensified, as it is in the modern world, by the ability of the few who direct labour--the labouring majority can never be free in their technical capacity of producers, they are free, and must always remain free, in respect of their tastes as consumers. In other words, demand is essentially democratic, while supply, in proportion to its sustained and enhanced abundance, is essentially oligarchic.

Now, that demand is essentially democratic, and depends on the tastes and characters of those by whom the demands are made, nobody will be inclined to deny. But if we turn our attention from society, taken as a whole, to the exceptionally able minority on whom the business of supply depends, we shall find that these men, in their turn, form similarly a small democracy in themselves, and make, as suppliers, their own demands also--a demand for an economic reward, or an amount of personal wealth, not, indeed, necessarily equal to the amount of wealth produced by them, but bearing a proportion to it which is, in their own estimation, sufficient. This demand made by the exceptional producer rests on exactly the same basis as does that of the average customer. It rests on the tastes and characters of the men who make it; and it is just as impossible for the many to decide by legislation that the few shall put forth the whole of their exceptional powers for the sake of one reward, when what they want is another, as it is for the few to make the many buy snuff when they want tobacco, or buy green coats when they want black.[16]

That such is the case will, to those who may be inclined to doubt it, become more evident if they consider with more attention than they are generally accustomed to exercise what the main attraction of great wealth is for the men who in the modern world are the producers of it on the greatest scale. Socialists and similar reformers--the people who principally busy themselves with discussing what this attraction is--are the people who are least capable of forming any true opinion about it. They not only have, as a rule, no experience of wealth themselves, but they are further generically distinguished by a deficiency of those powers that create it. They are like men with no muscles, who reason about the temperament of a prize-fighter; and their conception of what wealth means for those who produce and possess it is apt, in consequence, to be of the most puerile kind. It is founded, apparently, on their conception of what a greedy boy, without pocket-money, feels when he stares at the tarts lying in a pastry-cook's window. To them it seems that the desire for great wealth means simply the desire for purely sensual self-indulgence--especially for the eating and drinking of expensive food and wine. Consequently, whenever they wish to caricature a capitalist they invariably represent him as a man with a huge, protuberant stomach. The folly of this conception is sufficiently shown by the fact that many of the greatest of fortune-makers have, in their personal habits, been abstemious and even niggardly to a degree which has made them proverbial; and that, even in the case of those who value personal luxury, the maximum of self-indulgence which any single human organism can appreciate, is obtainable by a hundredth part of the fortunes for the production of which such men work. The real secret of the attraction which wealth has for those who create it lies in the fact that wealth is simply a form of power. These men are made conscious by experience, as less gifted men are not, that they can, by the exercise of their own mental energies, add indefinitely to the wealth-producing forces of the community. They feel the machine respond to their own exceptional management of it; they see the output of wealth varied and multiplied at their will; and thus the results of their specialised power as producers are neither more nor less than this same internal power converted into an external, an indeterminate and universalised form; and the reason why they will never produce wealth merely in order to be deprived of it is that no one will exercise power merely in order to lose it, and allow it to pass into the hands of other people. These men, as experience, especially in America, shows us, are constantly willing to use this power for the benefit of their kind generally; but this is no more a sign that they would be willing to allow it to be forcibly taken from them than the fact that a man is willing to give a shilling to a beggar in the street is a sign that he would allow the beggar to steal it out of his waistcoat-pocket.

So long as differences in personal power exist, especially in such power as affects the material circumstances of mankind, these differences in power, let governments take what form they please, will necessarily assert and embody themselves in the very structure of human society; and socialists are only able to obscure this fact from anybody either by a childish theory of modern production which they themselves are now repudiating, or else by a psychology even more laboriously childish, which would at once be exposed were it tested by so much as six months' experience. An interesting admission of the truth of this may be found in an unlikely place--namely, a work written some years ago by a socialist of considerable talent, which shows how the errors of at least a number of socialists are due, not to any defect in their reasoning powers, as such, but to a want of balanced knowledge of human nature in general, a want which in certain respects renders their reasoning futile. The work to which I refer is a work by a socialistic novelist, who was also an accomplished naturalist--the late Mr. Grant Allen. It is called The Woman Who Did.

The immediate object of the writer was to exhibit the institution of marriage as the cause of what he was pleased to regard as woman's degradation and slavery; and his heroine is a young lady of highly respectable parentage, who proposes to regenerate womanhood by living with, and having children by, a man, without submitting to the humiliation of any legal bond. She accomplishes her purpose, and has a daughter, whose position, under our false civilisation, becomes so disagreeable in consequence of her illegitimate birth, that the mother at last commits suicide, in order to deliver her from the presence of such an embarrassing parent. In the author's view she is a martyr, and a model for immediate imitation. Ludicrous, however, as the book is in its main scheme and in its object, the author shows great acuteness in a number of his incidental observations. He is, for example, constantly insisting on the fact that the institution of private property, which socialism aims at revolutionising, is merely one embodiment of a general principle of individualism of which marriage and the family are another, and that the two stand and fall together. But an admission yet more important than this is as follows: So that nothing may be wanting to the bitterness of the heroine's sublime martyrdom, the author represents her daughter--and he does this with considerable skill--as developing from her earliest childhood all those tastes and prejudices (an instinctive sympathy with those ordinary motives and standards) against which the mother's whole life, and her education of her daughter, had been at war. "Herminia," says Mr. Allen, "had done her best" to indoctrinate the child with the pure milk of the emancipating social gospel; "but the child herself seemed to hark back, of internal congruity, to the lower and vulgarer moral plane of her remoter ancestry. There is," he proceeds, "no more silly and persistent error than the belief of parents that they can influence to any appreciable degree the moral ideas and impulses of their children. These things have their springs in the bases of character; they are the flower of individuality; and they cannot be altered after birth by the foolishness of preaching." Let us read this passage, with the alteration of only a word or two, and it forms an admirable criticism of the more recent speculations of the party to which Mr. Allen belonged. There is no more silly and persistent error on the part of socialists than the belief that they can influence to any appreciable degree the moral ideas and impulses of the citizens of any community, or that these things, which are the flower of congenital individuality, can be altered after birth by the foolishness of socialism.

But the arguments at the service of socialism are not exhausted yet. Even if voting majorities should be unable to transform human nature, that men of power shall become willing to exert their power only in order that they may be deprived of it, there is a class of socialists who declare that what is impossible with mere human democracy, will be rendered possible by the divine influence of a rightly preached Christianity. To Christian socialists, as such, I have as yet made no special reference; nor will it be necessary now to be very prolix in our dealings with them; but in their attitude and their equipment for the task of effecting an economic revolution, they throw so strong a light on the character of contemporary socialism generally that a brief consideration of their gospel will be interesting and highly instructive, and will fitly lead us to the conclusion of this part of our argument.

FOOTNOTES:

[15] Mr. G. Wilshire, in his criticism of the argument, as stated by me in America, says that, under the existing system, the consumer is not free to choose what goods he will buy, but has them thrust on him by the capitalist producer. Yet he, and socialists in general, complain at the same time of the competition between capitalists, which is simply a competition to supply what consumers most desire. Here and there, when no competition exists, one firm can force its goods, if they are of the nature of necessaries, on the local public. But under the existing system this is only an occasional incident. Under socialism it would be universal. When tobacco is a state monopoly, state tobacco is forced on the great mass of the people.

[16] Mr. G. Wilshire admits, on behalf of socialists, that the argument of this chapter is so far correct that no democracy can make men of ability exercise their ability if they do not wish to do so; and that if they wish for exceptional rewards they will be able to demand them. A Melba, he says, under socialism, would be able, if she wished for it, to get probably even higher remuneration than she does to-day. But, he continues, under socialism, such men and women, though they could get such rewards, will be so changed that they will not wish for them. A Melba will then sing for the mere pleasure of singing.

CHAPTER XI

CHRISTIAN SOCIALISM AS A SUBSTITUTE FOR SECULAR DEMOCRACY.

Christian socialism, as a doctrine which is preached to-day, might, for anything that its name can tell us to the contrary, be as different from ordinary socialism as is Christian Science from secular--as the science of Mrs. Eddy is from the science of Mr. Edison. We can judge of it only by examining the utterances of its leading exponents. For this reason, although I had long been familiar with the utterances of persons who call themselves Christian socialists in England, I felt bound to decline an invitation to discuss the subject in America, unless I could be furnished with some recent and formal version of the gospel as it is preached there. Accordingly there was sent to me the precise kind of document I desired. It formed the principal article in a journal called The Christian Socialist. Its author was a clergyman,[17] and it was entitled "The Gospel for To-day." It was what I expected that it would be. It reproduced in almost every particular the thoughts and moods distinctive of Christian socialists in England; and this article I will here take as a text.

The writer, exhibiting a candour which many of his secular brethren would do well to imitate, starts with an attack on all existing forms of democracy, which are all, he says, based on a profound and fatal fallacy. This is the assumption that all men are born equal, from which assumption the practical conclusion is deduced that the best state of society is one which will allow each of these so-called equal beings to work out his own happiness as best he can for himself, with the minimum of interference from his fellow-citizens or from the law. Now if, says our author, men were born equal in reality, such an individualistic democracy might perhaps work well enough. But men are not born equal. The root of the difficulty lies here. In the economic sense, as in all others, some men are incomparably more able than the great majority of their fellows, and even among the exceptionally able some are much abler than the others. Consequently, if the principles of modern individualistic democracy and modern individualistic economics are right, according to which the main motive of each should be to do the best for himself with his own powers that he can--"if it is duty to compete if competition is the life of trade, then the battle for self must ever go grimly on. The strong must subdue the weak, the rich the poor, the able the unable. Upon this basis the millionaire and the multi-millionaire have a perfect right to roll up their untold millions, even as the working-man has a right to seek the highest wages that he can get. All in different ways are seeking their own; and the keenest competitors are the best men. The prizes must go to the strongest and the shrewdest. It is the survival of the fittest."

Such being the case, then, asks the writer, what does Christian socialism aim at? It does not aim at making men equal in respect of their ability, for to do this would be quite impossible; but it aims at producing an equality of a practical kind, by inducing the men whose ability is most efficient to forgo all personal claims which are founded on their own exceptional powers, so that the wealth which is at present secured by these powers for themselves may in the future be divided among the mass of their less able brethren.

Thus the crucial change which the Christian socialists would accomplish is identical with that contemplated by their secular allies or rivals. But the more completely it is invested with a definitely religious quality, the more lopsided, unstable, and self-stultifying is this change seen to be; the more obvious becomes the absurdity of proposing to reorganise the entire business of the world on the basis of a conversion de luxe which is to be the privilege of the few only, while the many are not only debarred, from the very nature of the case, from practising the renunciation in which the few are to find eternal life, but are actually urged to cherish their existing economic concupiscence, and raise it to a pitch of intensity which it never has reached before. The competent, to whose energies the riches of the world are due, are to put these riches away from them as though they were food offered by the devil. The incompetent, with thankless but perpetually open mouths, are to swallow this same food as though it were the bread from heaven. In other words, according to our Christian socialist, the sin against the Holy Ghost, which is involved in the enjoyment of riches, is not the enjoyment of material superfluities itself, but only the enjoyment of them by men who have been at the trouble of producing them.

That this is what the message of Christian socialism comes to, little as those who deliver it realise the fact themselves, is shown by an illustration obtruded on us by the author of "The Gospel for To-day." The evils of the existing situation, and its remoteness from the Kingdom of Christ, are, he says, exemplified in a very special way by the present position of the clergy. "If we churchmen," he says, "want money for our own purposes, we have to go to the trust magnates and kneel. We have to kneel to 'the steel kings and the oil kings,' merely because they are rich men." Now, how would Christian socialism alter a state of things like this? Let us consider precisely what it is that our Christian socialist complains about. He obviously does not mean that he and his brother clergymen have to approach the trust magnates on their knees. The utmost he can mean is that, if they want these men to give them money, they have to ask for it as a gift, and presumably make, when it is given, some acknowledgment to the donors. This it is which evidently sticks in the stomach of the humble follower of Christ whose self-portraiture we are now considering; for, if we confine ourselves to the Christian element in his teaching, he proposes to alter the existing situation only by kindling in the "trust magnates" such a fire of Christian philanthropy that they will have given him all he wants before he has had time to ask for it, thus exonerating him from the duty of saying "Thank you" for what he owes to another's goodness, and enabling him to offer to the Lord that which has cost him nothing.

And what the author of "The Gospel for To-day" urges on behalf of himself and his clerical brethren is precisely what he urges on behalf of the less competent majority generally. Neither on them nor on the Christian clergy does the gospel of Christian socialism urge the duty of making any new sacrifice, or any new exertion, moral or physical, for themselves. Just as the clergy are to learn no more of business than they know now, but are to be relieved of the necessity for all prudence as to ways and means, so is the ordinary labourer to work no longer, no harder, and no better than he does now. On the contrary, his hours of labour are to become ever less and less, and at the same time he is to receive ever greater and greater wages. These are to be drawn from the products, not of himself but of his neighbour: and although he will owe them solely to the virtue which his neighbour exercises, he is, according to the Christian socialist programme, to demand them as though his own incompetence gave him a sacred right to them.

Now, apart from the fact that this gospel does resemble the Christian in declaring that, while salvation can be achieved only by sacrifice, and that so far as the majority are concerned their sacrifice must be strictly vicarious, we might well pause to inquire how either of its two messages--that of economic asceticism for the few, and of economic concupiscence for the many--has any relation to the gospel of Christ at all. According to any reasonable interpretation of the words and spirit of Christ, a labourer's desire to enjoy the utmost that he himself produces is no less legitimate than natural; but it hardly ranks as one of the highest Christian virtues. How, we might ask, is it to acquire this latter character by being turned into a desire for what is produced by other people? Again, on the other hand, though according to most of the churches Christ did not condemn the possession of superfluous wealth as such, he certainly did not teach that the possession of it was generally necessary to salvation. It might therefore be justly urged, from the point of view of the few, that in proportion as Christ's valuation of this transitory life was accepted by them, the duty of melting down their own vases and candelabra in order that every workman's spoon might have a thin plating of silver on it, would constantly seem less and less, instead of more and more imperative. All this might be urged, and more to the same effect; but we will content ourselves with considering the matter under its purely practical aspect, and asking how any Christian clergymen--men presumably sane and educated--can propose, whether their programme be really Christian or no, to reorganise society on the basis of a moral conversion which is confined to the few only--which would exact from the able minority the maximum of effort and mortification, and secure the maximum of idleness and self-indulgence for the rest of the human race?

To this question it may be said that there are two answers. Admirable in character as are multitudes of the Christian clergy, nobody will contend that all of them are beyond reproach; nor will any such claim be made for all those of them who profess socialism. And for some of this body it is hardly open to doubt that the preaching of socialism is nothing better than a species of ecclesiastical electioneering. In the language of the political wire-puller, it affords them a good "cry" with which to go to the people. Why, they say in effect, should you listen to the agitator in the street, when we can give you something just as good from the pulpit? What the message really means which they thus undertake to deliver, they make no effort to understand. It will attract, or at least they think so; and for the moment this is enough for them. Having probably emptied their churches by talking traditional nonsense, they are willing to fill them by talking nonsense that has not even the merit of being traditional. We will not linger, however, over the case of men like these. We will turn to that of others who are morally very much more respectable, and whose condition of mind, moreover, is very much more instructive. Of these we may take the author of "The Gospel for To-day" as a type. He, we may assume, advocates his socialistic programme, not because he thinks that to do so is a shrewd clerical manoeuvre, but because he honestly believes that his programme is at once Christian and practicable. How does it come about, then, that an educated man like himself can believe in, and devote himself to preaching, doctrines so visionary and preposterous? Let us examine his arguments more minutely, and we shall presently find our answer.

By his vigorous denunciation of the doctrine that all men are born equal, he shows us that he is capable to a certain extent of seeing things as they are. But he sees them from a distance only, as though they were a range of distant mountains whose aspect is falsely simplified and constantly changed by clouds, and of whose actual configuration he has no idea whatever. Thus when he contemplates the inequalities of men's economic powers, these appear to him alternately in two different forms--as genuine powers of production and as powers of mere seizure--without his discerning where in actual life the operation of the one ends and the operation of the other begins: and, though for a certain special purpose he admits, as we shall see presently, that some able men are able in the sense of being exceptionally productive, his thoughts and his feelings alike through the larger part of his argument are dominated by the idea that ability is merely acquisitive. This is shown by the fact that the two great productive enterprises which he singles out as typical of modern wealth-getting generally are held up by him as examples of acquisition pure and simple. "The steel kings," he says, "did not invent steel. The oil kings did not invent oil." These are the gifts of nature, which nature offers to all; but the strong men abuse their strength by pushing forward and seizing them, and compelling their weaker brethren to pay them a tribute for their use. Steel and refined oil he evidently looks upon as two natural products. He has no suspicion that, as any school-boy could have told him, steel is an artificial metal which, as manufactured to-day, is one of the most elaborate triumphs of modern industrial genius. As to the oil by the light of which he doubtless writes his sermons, he apparently thinks of it as existing fit for use in a lake, and ready to be dipped up by everybody in nice little tin cans, if only the oil kings having got to the lake first, did not by their superior strength frighten other people away. Of the actual history of the production of usable oil, of the vast and marvellous system by which it is brought within reach of the consumers, of the by-products which reduce its price--all of them the results of concentrated economic ability, and requiring from week to week its constant and renewed application--the author of "The Gospel for To-day" apparently knows nothing. The oil kings and the steel kings, according to his conception of them, need merely refrain from the exercise of their only distinctive power--that is to say, an exceptional power of seizing; and every Christian socialist in New York and elsewhere will have the same oil in his lamps that he has now, and a constant supply of cutlery and all other forms of hardware, the sole difference being that he will get them at half-price or for nothing, and have the money thus saved to spend upon new enjoyments. And his conception of ability, as connected with the output of steel and oil, is his conception of ability as applied to the production of goods generally.

He makes, however, one exception. There is, he admits, one form of ability which does actually add to the wealth of the modern world, and may possibly be credited with producing the largest part of it. This is the faculty of invention. Here, at last, we seem to be listening to the language of sober sense. But let us see what follows. Inventors, our author proceeds, being the types of exceptional ability which is really beneficent and productive, are precisely the men who afford us our surest grounds for believing in the possibility of that moral conversion which socialism proposes to effect among able men at large. For what, he says, as a fact do we find the inventors doing? They invent, he says, for the pure love of inventing, or else from a desire to do good to their fellow creatures. The thought of money for themselves never enters into their minds. The selfish desire for money makes its appearance only when the strong man whose ability is merely acquisitive thrusts himself on the scene, buys the inventors' inventions up, and then proceeds "to work them for all they are worth." These mere seizers of wealth, these appropriators of the inventions of others, need but to learn a lesson of abnegation which the inventors have learned already, or rather a lesson which is easier; for while these noble men, the inventors, have no wish to take what they produce, the majority of able men, such as the steel kings and the oil kings, need merely forbear to take. Competition, in short, as it actually exists to-day--the competition which Christian socialism will abolish--is simply a competition in taking; and in order to abolish it, the strong men, when they have taken a fair share, have but to stand aside, to become as though they were weak, and so give others a chance equal to their own.

Here, indeed, we have a conception, or rather a vague picture, of the facts of modern industry, and of human nature as connected with it, which is worthy of a man from dreamland. Every detail mentioned is false. Every essential detail is omitted. In the first place, the disinterested inventor, from whose behaviour our author reasons, is purely a figment of his own clerical brain. Inventors in actual life, as every one knows who has had occasion to deal with them, are generally distinguished by an insane desire for money, by the wildest over-estimates of the wealth which their inventions will ultimately bring them, or by a greed which will sell them for a trifle, provided this be paid immediately. In the second place, inventions, even the greatest, so long as they represent the power of invention merely, are utterly deficient in all practical value. So long as they exist nowhere except in the author's brain, or drawings, or in descriptions, or even in the form of models, they might, so far as the world is concerned, have never existed at all. In the former cases they are dreams; in the last case they are toys. They are brought down into the arena of actual life only when, like souls provided with bodies, they cease to be ideas or toys, and become machines or contrivances manufactured on a commercial basis; and in order to effect successfully this practical transformation, countless processes and countless faculties are involved other than those comprised in intellectual invention itself.

There are cases, no doubt, in which the practical talents necessary for realising an invention and the faculty of invention itself coexist in the same man; but the inventor, when this happens, is not an inventor only. He is not only a master of ideas; he is a master of things and men. Such a combination is, however, far from common. As a rule, if his inventions are to be of any use to the world, the inventor must ally himself with men of another type, and these are the very men whom the author of "The Gospel for To-day" conceives of as simply monopolising and "working for all they are worth" contrivances which would otherwise have been given to the world gratis. He does not see that, if men such as the steel kings and the oil kings did not work inventions for all they are worth, the inventions themselves would be practically worth nothing.

Let the reader reflect on the astounding ignorance of the world, and especially of the world of industry, which is betrayed with so much na 風圍 et?by this socialist of the Christian pulpit. He knows so little of the commonest facts of history that he looks upon steel as a ready-made product of nature, and all the mills of the steel trust as merely a means of monopolising knives, bridges, rails, and locomotive-engines, which the citizens of America would otherwise be able to take at will, like a bevy of school-children helping themselves from a heap of apples. He imagines that inventions, as they form themselves in the head of the inventor, leap direct into use, without any intervening process; while the inventor himself is a being so superior to the world he works in, that the rapture of being allowed to work for it is the only reward he covets, that he has never dreamed of such selfish things as profits, and does not even know the meaning of a patent or a founder's share; and that the oil kings and the steel kings and all other able men, will save society by following in the footsteps of this chimera.

Such are the wild, childish, and disconnected ideas entertained by our clerical author of the world which he proposes to reform; and he is in this respect not peculiar. On the contrary he is a most favourable type of Christian socialists generally; and Christian socialists, in respect of their mental and moral equipment, are simply secular socialists of the more modern and educated type, with their ignorances and credulities accentuated, but not otherwise altered, by the solemnities of religious language, and a vague religious sentiment which achieves a facile intensity because it is never restrained by fact.

Socialists, in short, of all schools, are socialists because they are ignorant of, or fail to apprehend, certain facts or principles of nature and of human nature which are essential to the complicated process of modern productive industry; or it is perhaps a truer way of putting the case to say that they could not be socialists unless they were thus ignorant. In this they resemble the devisers of perpetual motions, or scientific and infallible systems for breaking the bank at a roulette-table. In so far as they are socialists--that is to say, in so far as they differ from other reformers--they are men aiming at something which is in its nature impracticable; and in order to represent it to themselves and others as practicable, they must necessarily ignore or fail to understand something which, in actual life, stands in the way of its being so. The perpetual-motionist believes that a perpetual motion is practicable, because he fails to see that out of no machine whatever is it possible to get more force than is put into it, and that one pound-weight will not wind up another. The system-monger sees that if a succession of similar stakes are placed on red or black, or any one of the thirty-six numbers, the bank always has zero in its favour; but by placing a number of stakes simultaneously in intricate combinations, or by graduating them according to results, he imagines that he can invert the situation, when all he can do is to disguise it. He often disguises it most effectually; but in the long run he does no more. Like a protuberance in an air cushion, which if pushed down in one place reappears in another, the original advantage of the bank infallibly ends in reasserting itself. The system-monger fails to see this for one reason only--that, having disguised, he thinks that he has eliminated, a fundamental fact of the situation. Socialists, in so far as they are socialists, reason in the same way. Though most of them now recognise, like the author of "The Gospel for To-day," that the economic efficiencies of men are in the highest degree unequal, they propose out of an inequality of functions to produce an equality of conditions. The details of the changes by which they propose to effect this result, or the grounds on which they seek to represent this result as possible, vary like the details of the systems of ingenious gamblers. But whatever these details may be, whether they are details of scheme or argument, the essential element of each is the omission of some fundamental fact--or, rather, of one protean fact--by which socialistic thinkers are often honestly confused, because it assumes, as they shift their positions, any number of different aspects. This is the fact that out of unequal men it is absolutely impossible to construct a society of equals.

Two illustrations, taken from the history of socialistic thought, will show how socialists hide this fact from themselves, first by a fallacy of one kind, then by a fallacy of another kind; and how, wherever it is located, it is the essential factor in their argument.

In their endeavour to prove the possibility of an equalisation, absolute or approximate, of economic conditions, Karl Marx and the earlier socialists started with two main doctrines. The one was a moral doctrine; the other was an economic. The moral doctrine was that, as a matter of eternal justice, every man has a right to the whole of what is produced by him. The economic doctrine was that, as a matter of fact, the only producers of wealth are the mass of manual labourers, and that, with certain unimportant exceptions, the economic values produced by all labourers are equal. Hence he argued that all wealth ought to go to the labourers, and that all labourers were entitled to approximately equal shares of it. The later socialists aim at reaching the same conclusion, and they start with two doctrines, a moral and an economic, likewise. Having arrived, however, at a truer theory of production--having recognised that labour is not the sole producer, and that some men produce incalculably more than others--they have, in order to support their demand for an equality of possession, been obliged to supplement their repudiation of the economic theory of their predecessors, by repudiating their theory of eternal justice also, and introducing another of a wholly opposite character. While Karl Marx contended that, in justice, production and possession were inseparable, the later socialists contend that there is no connection between them, and that it is perfectly easy to convert to this moral view every human being who is likely to suffer by its adoption. Thus the difference between the earlier and the later socialists is as follows: The earlier socialists started with a theory of justice which is in harmony with common-sense and the general instincts of mankind; and this theory was pressed into the service of socialism only by being associated with a false theory of production. The later socialists start with a truer theory of production; and they reconcile this with their own practical programme, only by associating it with a false moral psychology. In each case a fallacy is the basis of the socialistic conclusion; and without a fallacy somewhere--a fallacy which is pushed about, like a mouse under a table-cloth--no socialistic conclusion even tends to develop itself from the premises.

And what is true of the main arguments of the later, as of the earlier socialists, is equally true of their subsidiary arguments also, from those which refer to the generalisations of the sociologists of the nineteenth century, and base themselves on the confusion between speculative truth and practical, down to those which are drawn from the absurd psychological supposition that all motives are interchangeable, and that those which actuate the artist, the anchorite, and the soldier can be made to replace by means of a vote or a sermon those which at present actuate the masters of industrial enterprise. On whatever argumentative point the socialists, as socialists, lay stress, there, under one form or another, their root-fallacy reappears. In short, their arguments are illusionary in proportion as they themselves value them. And in this there is nothing wonderful. The more logically and ingeniously men reason from premises, of which the one most essential to their conclusions is radically false to fact, the more punctually on every critical occasion is this fallacy bound to reassert itself as the logical basis of that which they desire to prove.

The question, however, still remains to be answered of why a large body of men, like the educated apostles of socialism, who exhibit as a class no typical inferiority of intellect, unite in accepting, as though drawn to it by some chemical affinity, one particular error which dispassionate common-sense disdains, and which the actual history of the whole human race refutes? In the case of some preachers of socialism the answer lies on the surface. Socialism is of all creeds that which it is easiest to present to the ignorant; and in these days, like "patriotism" in the days of Dr. Johnson, it is often "the last refuge of a scoundrel," or of a desperate and ambitious fool. But I here put such cases altogether aside. What I here have in view are men who are morally and intellectually honest, and many of whom, indeed, are intellectually above the average. How is the affinity for one common error, and the passionate promulgation of it in forms, many of which are conflicting, to be accounted for in the case of men like these?

The answer to this is to be found, not in their intellect, but in their temperament. It is a well-known fact that men, otherwise of high capacity, are incapable of mastering any but the humblest branches of mathematics. With the men who become socialists the case is closely similar. Just as certain men are incapable of dealing with the abstractions of mathematics, so are the socialists men who, in virtue of their constitutions or temperaments, are incapable of comprehending accurately the concrete facts of life, and are consequently as unable with any practical accuracy, to reason about them as a professor of mathematics would be to reason about the value of strawberries, if he knew only their weights or numbers, but had no expert judgment with regard to their condition or quality.

To ascertain how the socialistic temperament thus debilitates the faculties, it will be enough to note certain characteristics distinctive of those possessing it. Such persons are all distinguished, though naturally in various degrees, by an undue preponderance of the emotional over the critical faculties, whence there arises in them what, to borrow a phrase of President Roosevelt's, we may aptly call an inflammation of the social sympathies. This makes such persons magnify into intolerable wrongs all sorts of pains and inconveniences which most men accept as part of the "rough and tumble" of life; and it thus renders them abnormally impatient of the actual, and abnormally preoccupied with the ideal. The ideal vision which they see arising out of the actual is for them so illuminated, as though by a kind of limelight, that the details of the actual, thrown into comparative obscurity, either cannot be minutely distinguished by them, or, like the words of an unwelcome talker, cannot fix their attention. Without habitual concentration of the attention on the subject-matter with which reason deals, no reasoning can deal with it to any practical purpose; and men of that class from which socialists of the higher kind are recruited, are men who fail to understand the modern industrial process, because they are hindered by their temperament from giving a sufficient attention to its details. They derive from them vivid impressions, but no practical knowledge, like Turner when he painted a train swathed in its own vapour, and flushing the wet air with the fires of its lamps and furnace. From a study of Turner's picture of "Rain, Steam, and Speed," it would be impossible for any human being to conjecture how a locomotive was constructed. It would be still more impossible to form any judgment as to how its slide-valves, or its blast, or the tubes of its boiler might be improved. It is similarly impossible for men of the socialistic temperament to understand the general process of industry, or to judge how it can and how it can not be altered, from the purely spectacular impressions which its intricate parts produce on them.

But the ingrained inability of such men to understand that which they would revolutionise does not reveal itself in their errors of theory only. It reveals itself still more strikingly in their own relations to life. If we allow for exceptional cases, such as that of Robert Owen, who was in his earlier days a competent man of business, we shall find that the theorists who desire to socialise wealth are generically deficient in the higher energies that produce it. Though they doubtless could, like most men who are not cripples or idiots, make a living by some form of manual labour, they have none of them done anything to enlarge the powers of industry, or even to sustain them at their present pitch of efficiency. They have never made two blades of grass grow where one blade grew before. They have never applied chemistry to the commercial manufacture of chemicals. They have never organised the systems or improved the ships and engines by which food finds its way from the prairies to the cities which would else be starving. If in some city or district an old industry declines they demand with tears that the thousands thus thrown out of employment shall be set by the state to do or produce something, even though this be a something which is not wanted by anybody. They never set themselves to devise, as was done in the English Midlands, some new commodity, such as the modern bicycle, which was not only a means of providing the labourers with a maintenance, but was also a notable addition to the wealth of the world at large. They fail to do these things for the simple reason that they cannot do them; and they cannot do them because they are deficient alike in the interest requisite for understanding how they are done, and in the concentrated practical energy which is no less requisite for the doing of them.

At the end of an address in which I had been dealing with this subject at New York, a young man, one of my hearers, told me that I had been putting into words what had long been borne in on himself by his own studies and observations--the fact, namely, that the social leaders of men are divided into two classes, _those who dream about reforming the industrial business of the world, and those, an opposite type, who alone advance and accomplish it_. Here we have the conclusion of the whole matter. These two classes are contrasted, not because in mere intellect one is inferior to the other, but because when they are dealing with the industrial affairs of life these affairs appeal to them in two contrasted ways. One of these classes takes men and nature as they are. With the utmost minuteness it masters the secrets of the latter, with the utmost minuteness it directs the actions of the former; and in seeking wealth for itself it brings about those conditions which alone can make added wealth a practical possibility for all. The other class, occupied not with what is but what ought to be, fails to understand what can be, because it does not understand what is. The men of whom this class is composed--the men whose temperamental deficiency now finds its fullest expression in socialism, as it did formerly in theories of ultra-democratic individualism, are like amateur architects, and amateur sanitary engineers, who, thinking in pictures, and having no knowledge of structure, condemn existing houses and existing systems of drainage, and would replace them with palaces which no builder could build, with arches which would collapse from the weight of their own materials, and magnificent cloac?the waters in which would have to run uphill.

The theory, then, of socialism, let it take what form it will--the theory which represents as practicable by one device or another the social equalisation of economically unequal men--is a theory which, in minds which are intellectually honest, can develop itself only in proportion as these minds are incapable of grasping in their connected completeness the actual facts of life; and that such is the case has been illustrated in the preceding chapters by a systematic analysis of all the crucial arguments on which socialists have rested their case from the earliest day of socialistic thought to the latest.

The reader, however, must observe the manner in which this statement is qualified. In speaking of the arguments of the socialists, I speak of those that are crucial only--that is to say, of those arguments used by socialistic thinkers in support of their programme in so far as that programme is peculiar. It is necessary to note this because, as a matter of fact, with such of their arguments as are proper to socialism only, the philosophers of socialism and their disciples frequently associate others which are not peculiar to the socialistic scheme at all, but which nevertheless multitudes of men who call themselves socialists regard as being at once the most important and practicable parts of it; and these I have in consequence reserved for separate treatment. They are three in number, and are as follows:

The first relates to the remuneration of the ordinary manual labourer, and deals with the question of what his just remuneration is. According to Marx this question is easily settled. Of every thousand labourers associated in any given industry, each produces, with few and unimportant exceptions, a thousandth part of the whole exchangeable product; and his just remuneration is a thousandth part of the value of it. The intellectual socialists of to-day, while repudiating as we have seen the doctrine that the labourer's claim to remuneration is limited to the values produced by him, and contending that he has a further right to the product of the ability of others, constantly declare that, even according to the moral standard of Marx, he is usually defrauded at present of a large part of his due; or that, in most if not all industries, his wages represent but a part of the full value produced by him. Whether this is so or not is a question not of theory but of fact, and one which can only be answered by discovering some intelligible basis on which the values produced by labour in a general way may be estimated, as distinct from those produced by effort of other kinds. With this question I shall deal in the following chapter.

The second relates to those forms of individual income which are covered by the word interest, when used in a comprehensive sense. It being admitted by the later socialists, in opposition to the earlier, that the directive ability of the few is, in the modern world, a productive agency no less truly than labour is, many of these socialists are now anxious to concede that the man of ability is entitled to such values, no matter how large, as are due to the active exercise of his own exceptional powers; but they contend that, as soon as his personal activity ceases, his claim to any influx of further wealth should therewith cease also. Let him spend his accumulations, they say, on his own gratifications as he will; but neither he nor his descendants can be suffered in moral justice to hold or apply them in such a manner that they will renew themselves, and yield an income to recipients who do nothing to make them fructify. To numbers of people who repudiate most of the socialistic programme, this doctrine as to interest appeals as at once just and practicable. If the state could appropriate all incomes due to interest, as distinct from those which represent the product of active ability, an enormous fund would, they think, be available for general distribution, and the ideals of socialism, in so far as they are practicable or desirable, might thus be realised by other than socialistic means. This argument, likewise, will have its own chapter--or rather two chapters--allotted to it.

The third of these arguments or proposals which, though not in themselves socialistic, are popularly associated with socialism, relates to equality of opportunity. To this also I will devote a separate chapter.

FOOTNOTES:

[17] While these pages were being corrected for the press, a number of utterances have been made by English clerics--Episcopalian and Nonconformist--precisely similar in purpose and spirit to those of the author here quoted.

CHAPTER XII

THE JUST REWARD OF LABOUR AS ESTIMATED BY ITS ACTUAL PRODUCTS

Since the educated socialists of to-day admit that in the modern world wealth is produced by two functionally different classes--a majority who labour and a minority by whom this labour is directed; or by two different faculties--namely, labour and directive ability--the question of how much of the total product or its value is produced by one class or agency, and how much by the other, is, for all social reformers, and not for socialists only, a question of the first importance; for in the minds of numbers, who care little about ideal transfigurations of society, the doctrines of socialism leave one vivid conviction, which is this--that, though the labourers in the modern world do not produce everything, though the ability of those directing them is a productive agent also, and though part of the wealth of modern nations is undoubtedly produced by this, yet the men of ability produce much less than they manage to keep, while the labourers produce much more than is represented by the wages which they get; that labour in this way, even if in no other, is suffering at present a general and intolerable wrong; and that socialism is simply a system by which this wrong will be righted.[18]

Now, this alleged wrong is essentially an affair of quantity. If the products of any typical firm--one, let us say, which produces chemicals--are represented by the number a hundred, and if fifty represents the amount which at present is the share of labour, the rest being taken by men of directive ability--a picked body of organisers, chemists, and inventors--labour, it is contended, produces more than the fifty, which is all that it at present gets. Yes; but how much more? It is not contended that it produces the entire hundred. Does it produce, then, sixty, or sixty-five, or seventy, or eighty-three, or what? Unless such a wrong as this can have some extent assigned to it--unless it can be measured approximately by reference to some intelligible standard--it is not only difficult to deal with it; it is impossible to be sure that it exists. Of course we are here not contemplating individual cases. That some employ 閡 may, under existing conditions, get less than their work is worth, is possible and likely enough. It is equally likely or possible that others may get more. We must confine ourselves to what happens generally. We must take labour as a whole, on the one hand, and directive ability on the other, and ask how we may estimate, with rough but substantial accuracy, the proportion of the joint product respectively produced by each.

At first sight it may seem that this problem is incapable of any definite solution; and some socialistic writers have done their best to obscure it. The efficiency of labour, they say, is in the modern world largely due, no doubt, to the action of directive ability; but ability could produce nothing unless it had labour to direct; whence it is inferred that the claim of labour on the product may in justice be almost anything short of the absolute total. To this abstract argument we will presently come back; but we will first examine another urged by a celebrated thinker, which, though less extreme in its implications, would, were it only sound, be even more fatal to our chances of arriving at the conclusion sought for. The thinker to whom I refer is Mill, who assigns to this argument a very prominent place in the opening chapter of his Principles of Political Economy.

Certain economists have, so he says, debated "whether nature gives more assistance to labour in one kind of industry than in another"; and he endeavours to show that the question is in its very essence unanswerable. "When two conditions," he proceeds, "are equally necessary for producing the effect at all, it is unmeaning to say that so much is produced by one, and so much by the other. It is like attempting to decide which of the factors five and six contributes most to the production of thirty." And if this argument is true of nature and labour, it is equally true of labour and the ability by which labour is directed. Thus a great ocean liner which, in Mill's language, would be "the effect," could not be produced at all without the labour of several thousand labourers; and it is equally true that it could not be produced at all unless the masters of various sciences, designers, inventors, and organisers, directed the labour of the labourers in certain specific ways. Both conditions, then, being "necessary for producing the effect at all," the portions of it due to each would, according to Mill's argument, be indeterminable. Let us consider, therefore, if Mill's argument is sound. We shall find that it is vitiated by a fallacy which will, as soon as we have perceived it, show us the way to the truth of which we are now in search. Let us begin with taking the argument as he himself applies it.

He brings it forward with special reference to agriculture, and aims it at the contention of a certain school of economists that nature in agriculture did more than in other industries. To urge this, says Mill, is nonsense, for the simple reason that though nature in agriculture does something, it is impossible to determine whether the something is relatively much or little. Let us, he says in effect, take the products of any farm, which we may for convenience' sake symbolise as so many loaves; and it is obviously absurd to inquire which produces most of them--the soil or the farm labourers. The soil without the labourers would produce no loaves at all. The labourers would produce no loaves if they had not the soil to work upon.

Now, if there were only one farm in the world, and one grade of labour, and if every acre of this farm, when the same labour was applied to it, would always yield the same amount of produce--let us say one loaf--Mill's argument would be true. The actual state of the case is, however, very different. Acres vary very greatly in quality; and if we take four acres of varying degrees of fertility, to all of which is applied the same amount of labour, then, while from the worst of the acres this labour will elicit one loaf, it will elicit from the others, let us say, according to their degrees of fertility, two loaves, three loaves, and four loaves respectively. Here the labour being in each of the four cases the same, and the additional loaves resulting in three cases only, it is obvious that the difference between the larger products and the less is not due to the labour, but to certain additional qualities present, in the three superior acres and not present in the worst one. In other words, although in producing loaves--or, as Mill describes it, "the effect"--the parts played by labour and nature are indefinite and incommensurable so long as the land, the labour, and the effect remain all three the same, the parts become immediately measurable when the effect begins to vary, and one of the causes, and only one of them, at the same time varies also.

This truth can be yet further elucidated by the very illustration which Mill cities in disproof of it. It is absurd to ask, he says, whether the number five or six does most, when they are multiplied together, to produce "the effect" thirty. This is true so long as "the effect" thirty is constant; but if on occasions the thirty is increased to forty, and if whenever this happens the six has increased to eight, we know that the extra ten which our multiplication yields us is not due to the five, the number which remains unchanged, but to an extra two now present in the number that was once six. Or again let us take as "the effect" the speed of a motor-car which is raced over a mile of road. Unless two conditions were present--the engine and some ground to run upon--the car could not run at all; and if there were only one road and one car in the world, it would be absurd to inquire how much of the speed was due to the merits of the engine, and how much to the character of the road's surface. But if, the car remaining unchanged, the surface of the road was improved, and a speed was thereupon developed of thirty miles an hour instead of twenty, we should, with regard to the increment, at once be able to say that it was due to the surface of the road, and was not due to the engine. Conversely, if the road were unchanged, but the car had a new engine, and the speed under these conditions increased in the same way, the increment would be evidently attributable to the engine and not the road.

And the same observations apply to labour and directive ability, whenever the operations of both are essential to a given product. If the ability and the labour were always inevitably constant, and the product as to quality and amount were similarly constant also, we could not say that so much or so little of the effect was due to one cause, and so much or so little to the other. If there were in the world only a thousand shipwrights, and these men, working always under the same director, always produced in a year one ship of an unchanging kind, we could not say which of its parts or how much of its value were due to the man directing, and which or how much were due to the men directed. But if for one year this director were to retire and another was to take his place, and, the same labourers being directed by this new master, the result was the production not of one ship but of two; and if, when the year was ended, and the old master came back again, the annual product once more was not the two ships but one, we could then say, as a matter of common-sense with regard to the year during which the two vessels were built, that the second vessel, whatever might be the case with the first, was due wholly to the ability of the master, and not to the labour of the men. In other words, the ability of the director of labour produces so much of the product, or of that product's value as exceeds what was produced by the labourers before their labour was directed by him, and would cease to be produced any longer as soon as his direction was withdrawn.

That in the case of any result which requires separable causes for its production, this method of allocating to these causes respectively so much of the result and so much of it only, is a method always adopted in all practical reasoning, may be seen by taking a result which is not beneficial but criminal. Twenty Russian labourers, all loyal to the Czar, are, let us say, employed to dig out a cellar under a certain street, and to fill it with cases which ostensibly contain wine. Subsequently, as the Czar is passing, he is killed by a huge explosion. It then becomes apparent that the so-called cellar was a mine, and the harmless-looking cases had really been filled with dynamite. Now, if all those concerned in the consummation of this catastrophe were tried, it is perfectly evident that the part played by the labourers would be sharply discriminated from that played by the man employing them; and, although they contributed something which was necessary to the production of the result, it would certainly have been admitted by General Trepoff himself that they had contributed nothing to its essential and criminal elements. It is equally evident that the increment of wealth which results from the obedience of labourers to injunctions which do not emanate from themselves, is produced by the man who gives the injunctions, and not by the men who obey them.

But here we must return to the argument, already mentioned in passing, which may be restated thus: A thousand labourers, directed by their own intelligence only, produce a product whose amount we will call a thousand. The same labourers are directed by a man of ability, and the product rises from one thousand to two. But if the production of this second thousand is to be credited to the man of ability on the ground that, were the ability absent, no second thousand would be produced, we may reach by the same reasoning a conclusion precisely opposite, and credit not only the first, but both the thousands to labour, on the ground that, if the labour were absent, nothing would be produced at all. The argument is plausible; and in order to understand its fallacy we must give our attention to a fact, not generally realised, which is involved in all practical reasoning about all causes whatsoever.

If we use the word "cause" in its strict speculative sense, the number of causes involved in the simplest effect is infinite. Let us take, for example, the speed of a horse which wins a race. Why does the speed of this horse exceed that of the others? We may in answer point to qualities of its individual organism. But these will carry us back to all its recorded ancestors--sires and dams for a large number of generations: and even so we shall have been taken but a small part of our way. The remotest of these ancestors--why were they horses at all? For our answer we must travel through the stages of organic evolution, till we reach the point at which animal and vegetable life were one. Had any of these antecedents been missing, the winning race-horse would not have won the race. Nor is this all. We have to include in our causes air, gravitation, and the fact that the earth is solid. No horse could win on turf which was based on vapour. But by all the thousands who witness a great race this whole mass of ulterior, though necessary, causes is ignored. The only causes which for them have any practical interest are those comprised in the organism of the winning horse itself. Who would contend that this horse had not won its own victory, on the ground that part of its own speed--a part which could not be calculated--was contributed by the crust of the earth, or the general constitution of the universe? Any one arguing thus would be howled down as a madman. Now, why is this? Why would the common-sense of mankind, in a practical matter like a race, instinctively exercise this kind of eclecticism, concentrating itself on certain causes and absolutely ignoring others? Such behaviour is not arbitrary. It depends on a principle inherent in all practical reasoning whatsoever. Let us see what this principle is.

When, with any practical purpose in view, we insist that anything is the cause of anything else, or produces anything else, we are always selecting, out of an incalculable number of causes, one cause or agency which, under the circumstances in view, may or may not be present; which a careless person may neglect to introduce; which an ignorant person may be persuaded to take away; or a recognition of which will influence human conduct somehow; while all other causes, which no one proposes to take away, or which no one is able to take away, are assumed by all parties, but they are not considered by anybody. Why should they be considered? Not only are they so numerous that no intellect could deal with them, but they have, since with regard to them there is no difference of opinion, no place in any practical discussion at all. If a ton of stone is to be placed on a piece of framework, men may reasonably discuss whether the framework is strong enough to bear it, or whether material is not being wasted in making it stronger than necessary. What will happen without an additional girder? Or what will happen if we take two girders away? Will the stone fall or not? These questions belong to the domain of practical reasoning because to take a girder away, or else introduce fresh ones, lies within the power of the disputants. But no practical men would think of complicating the discussion by calculating what would happen if they suspended the action of gravitation, in which case the stone would need no support whatever; for to suspend the action of gravitation is within the power of nobody. If two men are debating in the middle of the night at midsummer whether there is enough oil in the lamp to keep it alight till sunrise, they are debating a question of a strictly practical kind: for it rests with them to put in more oil or not. What will happen if they do not? That is the point at issue. But they neither of them would debate what would happen if the movement of the earth were retarded, and the midsummer morning were delayed till the hour at which it dawns in winter. They do not discuss this contingency, for they rightly assume it to be impossible, and consequently the discussion of it would have no practical meaning.

And now let us go back to the question of labour and ability; and we shall see, in the case of products to the production of which both are essential, that, while ability is the practical cause of all such amounts or values as exceed what would have been produced by labour if there were no ability to direct it, it cannot be claimed in any similar sense that all amounts and values are conversely produced by labour, which exceed what would have been produced by the action of directive ability, if no labour existed for such ability to direct.

The reason why labour, in this respect, differs from ability is as follows: Whether directive ability shall or shall not exert itself depends upon human volitions which, according to circumstances, are alterable, just as it depends upon alterable human volitions whether a framework of steel be constructed in this way or in that; or whether a lamp be replenished with oil or no. But whether ordinary manual labour shall or shall not exert itself, is not similarly dependent on human volition at all. Let a nation be organised, no matter on what principles, the majority of the citizens will have to labour in any case. The supposition of their labouring is bound up with the supposition of their existence. To suppose that the labourers as a whole could permanently cease to labour, is like supposing that they could exist and yet permanently cease to breathe. They can cease to labour for moments, just as for moments a man can hold his breath, as they do on the occasion of a strike; but they can do so for moments only. Except in a region where climatic conditions are exceptional, what makes men labour is not an employing class, but nature. Directive ability does not make them labour; it finds them labouring. It finds them like wheels which are driven by an eternal stream, and which must turn and turn for ever, until they fall to pieces. To inquire, then, what would happen if labour ceased to exert itself is like inquiring what would happen if the earth were to retard its diurnal motion, or if some natural force--for example, that of gravitation--were to strike work for the sake of intimidating the cause of all things. Such suppositions are for practical purposes meaningless. But with the directive ability of the few, as opposed to the directed labour of the many, the case is dramatically different. For while there never can be any question of the directive faculties of the few being left alone in a world where there is no labour--for in the case of the majority, nature, the eternal taskmaster, will always make labour compulsory, so long as stomachs want food and naked backs want clothing--there constantly has been, and there may be again, a question of whether this mass of ordinary human labour shall find any exceptional ability so developed and so organised as to direct it. In the earlier states of society no such ability was operative. In savage communities it is not operative now; and there is constantly a question, among modern civilised nations, whenever the security of social institutions is threatened, of the action of this faculty being temporarily suspended altogether, either because those persons possessing it are deprived of the motives without which they will not exert it, or else because the labourers individually, on one ground or another, are impatient of submitting themselves to the direction of any intelligences but their own.

In other words, when we are seeking to measure the products due respectively to directive ability and to labour, by computing what would happen if either of these agencies were withdrawn, the withdrawal of one of them--that is to say, of ability--can alone be taken as possible by any practical reasoner. We have before us practically two alternatives only. One is a condition of things under which the exceptional ability of the few directs and co-ordinates the labour of the average many. The other is a condition of things under which the labour of the average many has to exert itself with the same severe continuity, but is guided, co-ordinated, and stimulated by none of those special faculties which raise a few men above the general level of efficiency. When these special faculties are applied to the direction of average labour, the output of wealth increases. When their application is interfered with or ceases, the output of wealth declines; and in the only practical sense of the words "cause" or "producer," these faculties of direction, or the exceptional persons who exercise them, are the true causes or producers of the whole of that portion of wealth which comes into being with their activity, and disappears or dwindles with their inaction.

The practical validity of this method of computation has been formally recognised, though not completely understood, by some of the later socialists themselves. Mr. Webb, for example, and his associates, have admitted that, of the wealth of the modern world a considerable part consists of "the rent of business ability."[19] This way of expressing the matter is true so far as it goes. It expresses, however, one-half of the truth only. Mr. Webb and his friends mean that, if we take the world as it is, the products due to ability in any given industry consist of the quantity by which the products of one firm, because it is managed by a man of superior talent, exceed the products of another firm which differs from the first only in the fact that it is managed by another man whose talent is not so great. They assume as their starting-point, in every case, the presence of directive ability sufficient to organise the labourers in such a way that the products of the entire group shall provide the labourers with wages which are up to a certain standard, and a minimum of profit or of surplus values besides. This lowest grade of ability is one of the postulates of their argument, just as in calculating agricultural rent the first postulate of our argument is a lowest grade of land.

Now, in connection with many questions of a more or less limited kind, this assimilation of the products of superior ability to rent, and of ability of a lower grade to land which is practically rentless, will serve our purpose well enough. Between the two cases, however, there is a vast and underlying difference; and when we consider our present problem under its widest and most vital aspect, it is the difference, not the likeness, between them, which constitutes our main concern. The nature of this difference has been pointed out already. When we are discussing rent and agriculture, land is a necessary assumption, for unless there were land, there could be no agriculture at all; but there can be, has been, and still is in the world, abundance of labour without directive ability; and while it would be meaningless to ask what would happen to rent if all land disappeared, the question of what would happen to labour if all ability were in abeyance is precisely the question raised by all schemes of economic revolution, and one which has been constantly illustrated by the facts of economic history.

Of such facts we may take the following, picturesque example: In the eighteenth century the Jesuit Fathers in Uruguay succeeded in teaching the natives a variety of Western arts, among others that of watch-making, and so long as the Jesuits were on the spot to direct them the natives exhibited much manual skill. But when, owing to political causes, the Jesuits were driven from the country, the natives sank back into their previous industrial helplessness. The temporary efficiency of their labour had been due to the ability that directed it; and as soon as that ability was withdrawn, the labour, left to itself, shrank again to its old relative inefficiency. Now, here we have a case precisely analogous to that which we have to deal with when considering at the present day how much of the products of any civilised nation is produced by the labour of the average units of the population, and how much by the ability of the exceptional men directing them. It is not a question of how much this or that group of labourers, which is directed by a man of the highest grade of ability, produces in excess of the products of some similar group which is directed by another man whose ability is somewhat inferior; it is a question of how much the same nation would produce, if every director of other men's labour were withdrawn, and the present labouring units left to their own devices.

These two questions, though not mutually exclusive, differ as much as the question of why one of two balloons rises above the earth to a height of three miles and a furlong, while a second balloon reaches the height of three miles only, differs from the question of why either of them rises in the air at all. Mr. Webb and his friends, with their theory of the rent of ability, confine themselves to the first of these--namely, the question of why one balloon rises a furlong higher than the other. The real question which we have to deal with here is why both balloons lift their aeronauts at least three miles into the clouds, while other men who have no balloon to lift them can get no higher than the top of the church steeple. Or to come back to literal fact, our problem must be expressed thus: Let us take the present population of Great Britain or America, and, having noted the wealth at present annually produced by it, ask ourselves what would happen if some duly qualified angel were to pick out and kill, or otherwise make away with, every man, who, in virtue of his assimilated scientific knowledge, his inventive gifts, his constructive and practical imagination, his energy, his initiative, and his natural powers of leadership, was better able to direct others than the other nine were to direct themselves?

We cannot make this experiment in precisely the way described; but history will provide us with equivalents which are sufficiently accurate for our purpose. There are, for example, in the case of Great Britain, data which have enabled statisticians with a considerable degree of unanimity to estimate the values produced per head of the industrial population at various periods from the reign of Charles II. till to-day, and to reduce these values to comparable terms of money. Now, we need not insist too much on the accuracy of the figures in question; but one broad fact is unmistakably shown by them--that the product per head towards the close of the nineteenth century was, to say the least of it, from four to five times as great as it was towards the close of the sixteenth. To what, then, was this increase in industrial productivity due? It was not due to any change in the spontaneous workings of nature. It can only have been due to some change in the character of human effort--either in that of the effort of each separate manual labourer, or else in that of the men by whom the labour of others is directed. The average labourer, however, at the close of the nineteenth century did not differ, as an isolated labouring unit, from the average labourer as he was at the time of the fire of London. The increase in industrial productivity must therefore be necessarily due to a change in the ability of those by whom the labourers are organised and directed. And here a priori reasoning is confirmed by actual facts, for the change which has taken place in the class which directs the labour of others has been, during the period in question, of the most notorious and astonishing kind. That class had been progressively absorbing into itself, and concentrating on the conduct of industry, ambitions, intelligences, and strong practical wills, which formerly found their outlets in very different channels-- ecclesiastical, political, and more especially military. Man for man, then, industry became more productive, because to an increasing degree the ablest men of the nation concentrated their exceptional powers on directing the business of production; and any one who wished to push things to an extreme conclusion might contend that the entire amount--some four or five hundred per cent.--by which the product per head in the year 1880 exceeded the product per head some two hundred years before, was due to directive ability, and directive ability only; and that the labourers, in their capacity of labourers, had no claim whatsoever to it. We will, however, put the case in a much more moderate form. We will, for argument's sake, concede to self-directed labour all that increase in the values produced per head, which took place between the time of Charles II. and the general establishment in Great Britain of the modern industrial system, with its huge mills and factories, and its concomitant differentiation of the directing class from the directed--an event which had been securely accomplished at the beginning of the nineteenth century. In making this concession, we shall, indeed, be defying fact, and ignoring the improvements, alike in manufacture and agriculture, which had taken place during the hundred years preceding, especially during the last fifty of them, and which were solely due to a minority of exceptionally able men.[20] We shall thus be conceding to the labourer far more than his due. Certainly no one can contend that we concede too little.

Let us take, then, the beginning of the nineteenth century as our standing-point; and, assuming that labour was the sole producer then, compare its productivity per head with the productivity of industrial effort--of labour and ability combined--some eight or nine decades later. The labourers of Great Britain as a body, to the exclusion of all other classes, actually divided among themselves, about the year 1880, more wealth per head--something like forty-five per cent.--than would have been theirs if they had lived in the days of their own grandfathers, and been able to appropriate as wages the income of the entire country.

Let us, then, repeat the question which we asked just now. Where has this addition to the income of labour come from? That part of it is attributable to ability--the ability of the Watts, the Stephensons, the Arkwrights, the Bessemers, the Edisons, and so forth--nobody in his senses will deny. Can it be said that any of it is attributable to labour? The period now under consideration is so brief that this question is not hard to answer. It can easily be shown that man, as a labourer skilled or unskilled, has acquired individually no new efficiencies since--to say the least of it--the days of the Greeks and Romans. An ancient gem-engraver would to-day be eminent among modern craftsmen. The implements of the Roman surgeons, the proportional compasses used by the Roman architects, the force-pumps and taps used in the Roman houses--all things that could be produced by a man directing his own muscles--were produced in the Rome of Nero as perfectly as they could be produced to-day. To this fact our museums bear ample and minute witness; while the Colosseum and the Parthenon are quite enough to show that the masons of the ancient world were at least the equals of our own. If no advance, then, in the quality of manual labour as such has taken place in the course of two thousand years, it is idle to contend that its powers have increased in the course of eighty. But a still more remarkable proof that they actually have not done so, and that no such increase has contributed to the increase of modern wealth, is supplied by events belonging to these eighty years themselves. I refer to the policy pursued by the trade-unions of reducing the practical efficiency of all their members alike to the level which can be reached by those of them who are least active and dexterous. Bricklayers, for example, are forbidden by the English unions to lay, in a given time, more than a certain number of bricks, though by many of them this number could be doubled, and by some trebled, with ease. Now, although, from the point of view of those bodies who adopt it, such a policy has many advantages, and is perhaps a tactical necessity, this levelling down of labour to the minimum of individual efficiency is denounced by many critics as a prelude to industrial suicide, and the alarm which these persons feel is doubtless intelligible enough. It is, however, largely superfluous. The levelling process in question must of course involve a certain amount of waste; but its effect on production as a whole is under most circumstances inappreciable. Building as a whole is not checked by the fact that the best bricklayers may do no more than the worst. All kinds of commodities are multiplied, improved, and cheapened, while thousands of the operatives whose labour is involved in their production are allowed to attend to but one machine, when they might easily attend to three. In a word, while the unions have been doing their effective best to keep labour, as a productive agent, stationary, or even to diminish its efficiency, the product of industry as a whole exhibits an unchecked increase. And what is the explanation of this? Little as the trade-unions realise the fact themselves, their own policy is an object-lesson which supplies us with the simple answer. The answer is that the increase of modern wealth--certainly its increase during the past eighty years--has not been due to any change in the efficiency of labour at all; that labour is merely a unit which directive ability multiplies; that if in the year 1800 labour produced everything, and its total products then be expressed by the number five, the products of the industrial population would be five per head still, if ability, as a multiplying number, successively expressible by two and three and four, had not increased the quotient to ten, fifteen, and twenty; ability thus being the producer, not indeed of the five with which we start, but of all the increasing differences between this and the larger numbers.

To return then to definite facts, since in the year 1800 an equal division of all the wealth of Great Britain would have yielded to each family an income of eighty pounds, and since eighty years later an equal division of the total which was actually appropriated as wages by wage-paid labour alone, would have yielded to each labourer's family some twenty-five pounds in addition, the labouring class as a whole in Great Britain to-day, instead of receiving less than its labour produces, receives on the lowest computation from thirty to thirty-three per cent. more. Or, to put the matter otherwise, more than a fourth of its present income is drawn from a fund which would cease to have any existence if it were not for the continued activity of a specially gifted class, by whose brains the data of science are being constantly remastered and re-assimilated, and by whose energy they are applied to the minds and muscles of the many from the earliest hour of each working day to the latest. And what is true labour, its products, and receipts in Great Britain, is broadly true of them in America and all other countries also, where modern capitalism has arrived at the same stage of development.

We are, let me say once more, not here contemplating individual cases. Of the total wage-fund divided among the labourers in any given country, too much may be given to some men, and too little to others; but of every million pounds which a million of such men receive, some two hundred and fifty thousand are distributed well or ill, which have not been produced by the efforts of these men themselves, but are due to the efforts of a class which is definitely outside their own.[21] If, then, it is contended that the just reward of labour is that total of wealth which labour itself produces, the idea that labour, in respect of its pecuniary remuneration, is, under present conditions, the victim of any general wrong, is so far from having any justification in fact that it only touches fact at all by representing a direct inversion of it. Labour, as a whole, does not, under existing conditions, get less than it produces.[22] It gets a very great deal more. If, therefore, the claims of labour are based on, and limited to, the amount of wealth which is produced by labour itself--that is to say, the total which it would now produce were the faculties of the directing and organising minority paralysed--what labour, thus appropriating the entire product, would receive, would be far less, not more, than what it actually receives to-day. Instead of defrauding it of any part of its due, the existing system is treating it with an extreme and even wanton generosity.

Is it, then, here contended, many readers will ask, that if matters are determined by ideal justice, or anything like practical wisdom, the remuneration of labour in general ought henceforth to be lessened, or at all events precluded from any possibility of increase? Is it contended that the employing and directing class should attempt or even desire to take back from those directed by it every increment of wealth possessed by them which is not produced by themselves? If any one thinks that such is the conclusion which is here suggested, let him suspend his opinion until, as we shall do in another chapter, we return to the subject and deal with it in a more comprehensive way. Our conclusion, as for the moment we must now be content to leave it, is not that the labourers have not a claim, practically valid, to the only portion of their income which has any tendency to grow, but merely that they should understand the source from which this portion is drawn--a source which consists of the efforts of other men, not of their own.

And now, before we return to this particular question, we will go on to deal with another which to a certain extent overlaps it, but is narrower in its compass, and seems, for that very reason, to many minds of greater practical moment. I mean the question of interest, or the income which comes to its recipients without any necessary effort on their own part to correspond to it.

FOOTNOTES:

[18] I met an interesting embodiment of this mood of mind in America, in the person of a slim young man, well-dressed, well-educated, refined in his speech and manners, who worked as a clerk or accountant in some large financial house. To my great astonishment he introduced himself to me as a socialist. "I don't believe like Marx," he said, "that labour produces everything, but I maintain that the task-work of the employed and directed labourer, of whatever grade--whether he uses a pen or a chisel--is always worth more than the wages which the employers pay him for performing it. I feel this myself with regard to my own firm. Month by month I am worth to it more than the sums it gives me. This," he went on, with an odd gleam in his eyes, "is what I may not endure to think of--that others should be always appropriating values which I have produced myself; and nine out of ten of the men who become socialists, do so because they feel as I do about this particular point."

[19] General Walker also seeks to assimilate the product of ability to rent; and my criticism of Mr. Webb in this respect applies to him also. General Walker's book was mentioned frequently in connection with my late addresses in America; and it was said by one or two critics that I had borrowed from, and ought to have acknowledged my debt to, him. As a matter of fact, I never saw his book till after my return to England, when I read it with interest and admiration. His doctrines with regard to the entrepreneur is, so far as it goes, fundamentally identical with the main argument of this volume. My criticism of him would be that he does not give to this particular part of his doctrine the foremost place which logically belongs to it; and that though attributing to the entrepreneur some special productive faculty distinct from labour, he starts his work with re-enumerating the old doctrine that labour, capital, and law are the only factors in production.

[20] For example, the silk factory at Derby, erected by Lombe, in the reign of George II., the machinery of which comprised 26,000 wheels.

[21] These figures represent less than the truth. They are merely given in order to indicate the general character of the situation to-day, as compared with that of an earlier, but still comparatively recent period. To go into details minutely would involve extensive and here needless discussion.

[22] A letter was sent me by a friend in America, from a writer who, commenting on my late addresses in that country, said that in the main he entirely agreed with my arguments, as against socialism; but that he could not divest himself of the belief that labour as a whole got less than it produced, and was thus as a whole suffering a chronic wrong. He suggested, however, a method, fundamentally analogous to that set forth in the text, of computing what labour, as such, does produce in reality. He gave his own opinion as to actual facts, as an impression merely; but how misleading impressions may be can be seen from his statements "that all very great fortunes, at all events, must be derived from the underpayment of labour." Had he only considered the case in detail, he would have seen that labour received the highest wages from some of the richest employers. According to his theory the wages of labour, in such cases, would touch the minimum.

CHAPTER XIII

INTEREST AND ABSTRACT JUSTICE

The essential feature of interest, as distinct from the income due to active ability, is that while the latter ceases as soon as the able man ceases to exert himself, the former continues to replenish the recipient's pockets, though for his part he does nothing, or need do nothing, in return for it. Since, then, the possession of this particular form of income is admittedly unconnected with any concurrent exertion on the part of those possessing it (such is the argument of the objectors) the whole portion of the national wealth which, in the form of interest, is at present appropriated by the presumably or the possibly idle, might obviously be appropriated by the state, and applied to public purposes, without lessening in any way even the highest of those rewards which are due to, and are needed to stimulate any active ability whatsoever, and hence without lessening the efficiency of the wealth-producing process as a whole. If we adopt the programme which this argument suggests, it will be possible, so its advocates say, to satisfy the demands of labour by a shorter and more direct method than that of committing ourselves to an estimate of what labour actually produces, and endeavouring to secure that the total which is paid to labour shall accord with it.

Now, this programme raises two separate questions. One question is whether the proposed confiscation of interest is in reality, as its advocates maintain it to be, practicable in the sense that the disturbances which it would necessarily cause would not interfere with the production of the fund which it is desired to distribute, and so perhaps leave all classes poorer and not richer than they are. The other question is whether such a confiscation would be just. To some people this second question will possibly seem superfluous. If it can be shown, they will say, that a policy, the avowed object of which is the enrichment of the many at the expense of the relatively few, could be really carried out successfully, and if the many had the power of insisting on it, an inquiry into its abstract justice is merely a waste of time; for whenever the wolf is face to face with the lamb, it will eat up the lamb first and justify its conduct afterwards. And in this argument there is a certain amount of truth; but those who take it for the whole truth allow their own cynicism to overreach them. The fact remains that even the wolves of the human world are obliged to assume, as a kind of necessary armour, and often as their principal weapon, a semblance of justice, however they may despise the reality. The brigand chief justifies his war on society by declaring that society has unjustly made war on him. The wildest demagogues, in their appeals to popular passion, as the history of the French Revolution and of all revolutions shows us, have always been obliged to exhibit the demands of mere self-interest as based on some general theory of what is morally just or right; and however much the theory may accommodate itself to the hope of private advantage, there are few demands made for any great social change which do not derive a large part of their force from persons with whom a belief in the justice of the demands stands first, while--so far at least as their own consciousness is concerned--the prospect of personal advantage stands second or nowhere. This is certainly so in the case which we are now considering. We will, therefore, begin with the question of abstract justice.

Let us begin, then, with reminding ourselves that when interest is attacked as such, on the ground that its recipients have themselves done nothing to produce it, whereas other incomes, no matter how large, are presumably the equivalents of some personal effort which corresponds to them, it is assumed that every man has, in natural justice, a right to such wealth as he actually himself produces; and what he produces, as we saw in the last chapter, is that amount of wealth which would not have been produced at all had his efforts not been made, or been other or less intense than they have been.

Thus far, then, for the purposes of the present discussion, all parties are agreed; but the moment the assailants of interest take the next step in their argument, we shall find that their errors begin--errors resulting, as we shall see, from an imperfect analysis of facts. For them the two types of correspondence between productive effort and product are, firstly, the manual labourer, who performs some daily task such as riveting plates or bricklaying, and receives an equivalent in wages at the end of each day or week; and, secondly, the manager of some great industrial enterprise, who spends each day so many hours in his office, issuing minute directions with regard to the conduct of his subordinates, and sending his receipts to the bank as they come in from his customers. But these types, though accurate so far as they go, do but cover a part of the actual field of fact. Practically, though of course not absolutely, they ignore the element of time. They represent effort and product as being always so nearly simultaneous that, although the former must literally precede the latter, yet, if we estimate life in terms of years, or even months, or weeks, a man has ceased to produce as soon as he has ceased to work.

Now, of certain forms of effort this may be true enough. A bricklayer, for example, as soon as he ceases to lay bricks, ceases to produce anything. His wall-building closes its effects with the walls which he himself has built. It does nothing to facilitate the building of other walls in the future. Similarly such ability as consists in a gift for personal management often ends its effects, and leaves no trace behind it, as soon as the manager possessing these gifts retires.

But with many forms of ability the case is precisely opposite. The products of their exercise do not even begin to appear till after--often till long after-- the exercise of the ability itself has altogether come to an end. Let us, for example, take the case of a play; and since socialists are still included among the objectors whom we have in view, let us take one of the popular plays written by Mr. Bernard Shaw. Such a play, as Mr. Shaw has publicly boasted-- for otherwise I should not mention, and should know nothing of his private affairs--brings to its author wealth in the form of amazing royalties; but until it is acted it brings him no royalties at all, and the actors begin with it only when his own efforts are ended. Moreover, not only do these royalties only begin then, but having once begun, they have no tendency to exhaust themselves. On the contrary the chances are that they will go on increasing till the time arrives, if it ever does, when Mr. Shaw is no longer appreciated. Mr. Shaw, in fact, if he had written one of his most successful plays at twenty, might, so far as that play is concerned, be idle for ever afterwards, even if he lived to the age of Methuselah, and still be enjoying in royalties the product of his own exertions, though he had not exerted himself productively for some seven or eight hundred years.

There is no question here of whether, under these conditions, a person like Mr. Shaw might not feel himself constrained on some ground or other to surrender his copyright at some period prior to his own demise. The one point here insisted on is that he could not renounce it on the ground that the wealth protected by it was no longer produced by himself. If he is entitled to the royalties resulting from the performance of his play at any time, on the ground that every man has a right to the products of his own exertions, his right to the royalties resulting from its ten-thousandth performance is, on this ground, as good as his right to the royalties resulting from the first. The royalties on a play, in short, show how certain forms of effort, though not all, continue to yield a product for an indefinite period, though the original effort itself may be never again repeated; and herein these royalties are typical of modern interest generally. They do not, however, constitute in themselves more than a small part of it. We will therefore turn to interest of other kinds, the details of whose genesis are indeed widely different, but which consist similarly of a constant repetition of values, without any corresponding repetition of the effort in which the series originated.

Those which we will consider first are the products of organic nature, which have been dwelt upon by a well-known writer as showing us the ultimate source of industrial interest generally, and also at the same time its natural and essential justice. It may be a surprise to some to learn who this writer is. He is Henry George, who is best known to the public as the advocate of a measure of confiscation so crude and so arbitrary, that even socialists have condemned it as impracticable without serious modifications. Henry George, however, although he outdid most socialists in his attack on private wealth of one particular kind--that is to say, the rent of land--was equally vehement in his defence of the interest of industrial capital. Socialists say--and the aphorism is constantly repeated--"A man can get an income only by working or stealing; there is no third way." In answer to this, it was pointed out by George that one kind of wealth, at all events--and we may add that here we have wealth in its oldest form--consists of possessions yielding a natural increase, which has been neither made by the possessors, nor yet stolen by them from anybody else. That is to say, it consists of flocks and herds. A shepherd or herdsman starts with a single pair of animals, from which parents there arises a large progeny. This living increment has not been produced by the man, but it is still more obvious that it has not been produced by his neighbours, and it therefore belongs in justice to the man who owns the parents. George pointed out also that whole classes of possessions besides are, for by far the larger part of their value, equally independent either of corresponding work or of theft. Among such possessions are wines, whose quality improves with time, and which, if sold to-day, may be worth tenpence a bottle, but which four years hence may be worth perhaps half-a-crown. In all such cases--this was George's contention-- we have some possession originally small to start with, which year by year is increased in amount or at least in value, not by the efforts of the possessor, but by the secret operations of nature. Here, he argued, we have capital in its typical form; and interest is the gift of nature to the man by whom the capital is owned.

George, however, is constrained to supplement this proposition by another. Though he assumes that of the products which are, in the modern world, actually paid as interest by the borrower of capital to the owners of it, the larger part consists of gifts of unaided nature, he admits that they are not the whole. He admits that a part of it is paid for the use of machinery. Now, such interest, he says, has a definitely different origin, and cannot intrinsically be justified in the same way; and if all wealth consisted of such commodities as are due to the efforts of man, and to the man-made machinery which assists him, all interest would be really, as it is said to be by some, indefensible. But, he continues, since interest on capital such as machinery is not the whole of the interest paid in the modern world, but is only a minor part of it, and since in the modern world all forms of capital are interchangeable, the laws which govern us in our dealings with the lesser quantity must necessarily be assimilated to those which govern us in our dealings with the greater. If a ram and a sheep are capital which yields just interest, because their wool and their progeny are increments due to nature, and if a ram and a sheep are exchangeable for some kind of machine, the possession of the one must be placed on a par with the possession of the other. The machine must be treated, though it is not so in strictness, as if it were prolific in the same sense as the beasts are; and a part of what it is used to produce must be paid by the user to the owner of it.

Now, both these arguments--that which deals with the fact of natural increase, and that which deals with the assimilation of all such possessions as are interchangeable--are in principle sound. The first, indeed, touches the very root of the whole matter; but the first is exaggerated in his statement of it, and unduly limited in his application, and the second is wholly unnecessary for proving what he desires to prove. The first is exaggerated in his statement of it because, as a matter of fact, the kind of capital whose interest is described by him as the gift of nature is not the major, it is only a minor part of the capital yielding interest under the conditions which obtain to-day. A part far larger is capital in the form of machinery; and if the distinction which George draws between the two is a true one, the case of the flocks and herds should be assimilated to that of the machines, not the case of the machines to that of the flocks and herds. Interest should be denied to both kinds of capital because machines are not naturally prolific, instead of being conceded to both because flocks and herds are so. We shall find, however, that the distinction which George seeks to establish is illusory, that both kinds of capital yield interest in the same way, and that his justification of it in the one case is equally applicable to it in the other.

His attempt to distinguish between the two takes the form of a criticism of Bastiat, according to whom the typical source of interest is the added productivity which a given amount of human effort acquires by the use of certain lendable implements. As a type of such implements or machines, Bastiat takes a plane. The maker of a plane lends this plane to another man, who is thus enabled to finish off in a week four more planks than he could have done had he used an adze. If, at the end of the week, the borrower does nothing more than return the plane in good repair to the lender, the borrower gains by the transaction; but the maker and lender not only gains nothing, he loses. For a week he loses his implement which he otherwise might have used himself, and the extra planks which, by the use of it, he could have produced just as easily as his fellow. Such an arrangement would be obviously and absurdly unjust. Justice demands--and practice here follows justice--that he get at the end of the week, not only his own plane back again, but two of the extra planks due to its use besides. A plane, in short--such is Bastiat's meaning, though he does not put it in this precise way--is a possession which is fruitful no less than a sheep and a ram are, or a wine which adds to its value by the mere process of being kept, and it, therefore, yields interest for a virtually similar reason. George, however, seeks to dispose of Bastiat's argument thus: If the maker of the plane lends it, he says, instead of himself using it, and the borrower borrows a plane, instead of himself making one, such an arrangement is simply due to the fact that both parties for the moment happen to find it convenient. For, George observes, it is no part of Bastiat's contention that the plane is due to the exertion of any faculties possessed by the maker only. Either man could make it, just as either man could use it. Why, then, should A pay a tribute to B for the use of something which, to-morrow, if not to-day, he could make for himself without paying anything to anybody?

Now, if Bastiat's plane is to be taken as signifying a plane only, the criticism of George is just. But what George forgets is that, if the plane means a plane only--an implement which any man could make just as well as the lender-- interest on planes, besides being morally indefensible, would as a matter of fact never be paid at all. Bastiat's plane, however, stands for a kind of capital, the borrowing of which and the paying of interest on which, form one of the most constant features of the modern industrial world; and he evidently assumes, even if he does not say so, that for all this borrowing and paying there is some constant and sufficient reason. Now, the only reason can be-- and George's own criticism implies this--that in order to produce the machine-capital borrowed certain faculties are needed which are not possessed by the borrowers; and though this may not be true of a simple hand-plane itself, it is emphatically true of the elaborate modern machinery of which Bastiat merely uses his hand-plane as a symbol. In order to produce such implements of production as these, the exertion of faculties is required which are altogether exceptional, such as high scientific knowledge, invention, and many others. Let invention--the most obvious of these--here do duty for all, and let us consider, for example, the mechanism of a modern cotton mill, or of a boot factory, or a Hoe printing press, or a plant for electric lighting. All these would be impossible if it had not been for inventive faculties as rare in their way as those of a playwright like Mr. Shaw.

No one will deny that when a play like "Man and Superman" first acquires a vogue which renders its performance profitable, the royalties paid to the author are values which he has himself created, not indeed by his faculties used directly, but by his faculties embodied in a work which he has accomplished once for all in the past, and which has thenceforward become a secondary and indefinitely enduring self; and if this is true of the royalties resulting from its first profitable performance, it would be equally true of those resulting from the last, even though this should take place on the eve of the Day of Judgment. With productive machinery the case is just the same. If Mr. Shaw, instead of writing "Man and Superman," had been the sole inventor of the steam-engine, and the only man capable of inventing it, every one will admit that he would, by this one inventive effort, have personally co-operated for a time with all users of steam-power, and been part-producer of the increment in which its use resulted. And if this would have been true of his invention when it was only two years old, it would be equally true now. He would still be co-operating with the users of every steam-engine in the world to-day, and adding to their products something which they could not have produced alone.

Here, then, we see that in one respect at all events the two kinds of capital, which George attempts to contrast, yield interest for a precisely similar reason. Both consist of a productive power or agency which is external to the borrower himself; and it makes no difference to him whether the auxiliary power borrowed inheres in living tissue, or in a mechanism of brass or iron.

But the resemblance between these two forms of capital, and the identity of the reasons why both of them bear interest, do not end here. I quoted in a former chapter an observation of Mr. Sidney Webb's, which he himself applies in a very foolish way, but which is obviously true in itself, and in the present connection is pertinent. Some men he admits are incomparably more productive than others, because they happen to be born with a special kind of ability. But what is this ability itself? It is simply the result, he says, of a process which lies behind them--namely, the natural process of animal and human evolution; and its special products are like those of exceptionally fertile land. That is to say, the ability which produces modern machines is in reality just as much a force of nature as that which makes live-stock fertile, and brings raw wine to maturity. But the same line of argument will carry us much farther than this. As Dr. Beattie Crozier has shown in his work, The Wheel of Wealth, the part which nature plays in productive machinery is not confined to the brains of the gifted inventors and their colleagues. It is incorporated in, and identified with, the actual machines themselves. The lever, the cam, the eccentric, the crank, the piston, the turbine, the boiler with the vapour imprisoned in it--devices which it has taxed the brains of the greatest men to elaborate and to co-ordinate--were all latent in nature before these men made them actual; and when once such devices are actualised it is nature that makes them go. There is not merely a transformation of so much human energy into the same amount of natural energy; but nature adds to the former a non-human energy of her own; as--to take a good illustration of Dr. Crozier's--obviously happens in the case of a charge of gunpowder, which, "when used for purposes of blasting, has," he observes, "in itself a thousand times the quantity of pure economic power that is bought in the work of the labourers who supply and mix the ingredients." That is to say, whenever human talent invents and produces a machine which adds to the productivity of any one who uses it with sufficient intelligence, the inventor has shut up in his machine some part of the forces of nature, as though it were an efreet whom a magician has shut up in a bottle, and whose services he can keep for himself, or hand over to others. The efreets shut up in machinery will not work for human beings at all, unless there are human magicians who manage thus to imprison them. They therefore belong to the men who, in virtue of their special capacities, are alone capable of the effort requisite to perform this feat; and it matters nothing to others, by whom the efreets' services are borrowed, whether the effort in question occupied a year or a day, or whether it took place yesterday or fifty years ago.

The borrowed efreet produces the same surplus in either case, and interest is a part of this surplus which goes, not to the efreet himself (for this is not possible), but to his master, just as a cab-fare is paid to the cabman and not his horse.

Machine-capital, then--or capital in its typical modern form--consists of productive forces which are usable by, and which indeed exist for, the human race at large, because, and only because, they have been captured and imprisoned in implements by the efforts of exceptional men, whose energy thus exercised is perpetuated, and can be lent to others; and what these men receive as interest from those by whom their energy is borrowed, is a something ultimately due to the energy of the lenders themselves--nor is this fact in any way altered by lapse of time. Thus, so far as these special men are concerned, the alleged difference between earned income and unearned altogether disappears; and if one man lives in luxury for sixty years on the interest of an invention which it took him but a month to perfect, while another man every day has to toil for his daily bread, the difference between the two consists not in the fact that the one man works for his bread and the other man does nothing for it, but in the fact that the work of one produces more in a day than that of the other would do in a hundred lifetimes.

Here, however, we shall be met with two important objections. In the first place, it will no doubt have occurred to many readers that throughout the foregoing discussion we have assumed that the persons who receive interest on machinery are in all cases the persons by whom the machinery was invented and produced. To the actual inventors and producers it may, indeed, be conceded that the interest which they themselves receive has been earned by their own exertions; but no such concession, it will be said, can be made to these men's heirs. An Edison or a Bessemer may have produced whatever income has come to him in his latest years from the inventive efforts of his earliest; but if such a man has a son to whom this income descends--a half-witted degenerate who squanders it on wine and women, who will not work with his hands and who cannot work with his head--no one can pretend that, in any sense of the word, a fool like this produces any fraction of the thousands that he consumes. And though all of those who live on the interest of inherited capital are not foolish nor vicious, yet in this respect they are all of them in the same position--they have not produced their incomes, and so have no moral right to them.

In the second place, the following argument, which was discussed in an earlier chapter, will also be brought forward, refurbished for the present occasion. Let us grant, it will be said, that the inventions which have enriched the world were originally due to the talents of exceptional men, and that without these exceptional men the world would never have possessed them; but when once they have been made, and their powers seen in operation, the human race at large can, if left to itself, take over these powers from the inventors just as the inventors took them over from nature. Indeed, this constantly happens. Any boy with a turning-lathe can to-day make a model steam-engine, and no one will contend that such a model was not made by himself, on the ground that it could not have been made either by him or by anybody unless Watt, with his exceptional genius, had invented steam as a motive-power. One might as well contend that a savage does not really light his own fire, on the ground that the art of kindling wood was found out by Prometheus, and that no one, except for him, would have had any fires at all. The truth is, it will be said, that in such cases as these the powers of the exceptional man, originally confined to himself, are, when his invention is once in practical operation, naturally shared by his fellows, who can only be restrained from using them by artificial devices such as patents--these devices being at best, from a moral point of view, devices by which one man who has given a cheque to another man steals back half the money as soon as the cheque is cashed.

Now, both these arguments, so far as they go, are true; but neither has any bearing on the problem which is now before us. That problem arises--let me observe once more--out of the assumption that, as a matter of justice, every man has a right to the products of all such forces as are his own; whence it follows that nobody has a right to the products of any forces which are not definitely in himself. Let us take, then, the latter of the above arguments first. It would doubtless be absurd to contend, were Prometheus alive to-day, that because he invented the art of striking fire from flints he ought to be paid a tribute by every savage who boiled a kettle; for the savage can strike a flint as well as Prometheus himself could. But if fire could be kindled only by a particular sort of match which Prometheus alone could make, the fact that he was really the lighter of all fires would be obvious, and his claim to a payment in respect of the lighting of every one of them would be as sound as the claim of the lighter of street-lamps to his wages. If "Man and Superman" were not a play, but a hoot, which Mr. Shaw had invented in order to call attention to himself, and which any street boy could imitate with the same results, it would be idle for Mr. Shaw to claim a right to royalties from the street boys; but it would be idle only because it would not be possible to collect them. He is able to collect them on his play because, and only because, his play exists in a form which is susceptible of legal protection. If in justice he has a right to these, as he no doubt has, he would, if abstract justice were the sole determining factor, have an equal right to royalties on the use of his peculiar hoot. He fails to have any such right because, as a matter of fact, the principle of abstract justice with which we are here concerned--that every one has a right to everything that he himself produces--has, in common with all abstract moral principles whatsoever, no application to cases in which, from the nature of things, it is wholly impossible to enforce it.

And the same criticism is applicable to the other argument before us, which admits that a man who invents a productive machine, or who writes a remunerative play, is, so long as he lives, entitled, because he is the true producer of them, to certain profits arising from the use of either; but adds that his rights to such profits end with his own life, and lose all sanction in justice the moment they are transferred to an heir. In the heir's hands, it is urged, they entirely change their character, and, instead of enabling a man to secure what is honestly his own, become means by which he is enabled to steal what morally belongs to others.

Now, if it is seriously contended that nobody has a right to anything which at some time or other he has not personally produced, the interest on machinery, as soon as the inventor dies, not only ought not to belong to the inventor's heir, but it ought not to belong to anybody; for if this interest is not produced by the heir, it is certainly not produced by any of the heir's contemporaries. A contention like this is absurd; there must therefore be something amiss with the premises which lead up to it. Socialists who admit that an inventor during his lifetime has a right to the interest resulting from the use of his own inventions, endeavour to solve the difficulty by maintaining that after his death both invention and interest should pass into the hands of the state; but this doctrine, on whatever grounds it may be defended, cannot be defended as based on the principle now in question, that the sole valid title to possession is personal production. It must, if it is based on any abstract moral principle at all, be based on one of a much more general kind, according to which the ultimate standard of justice is not the deeds of the individual, but the general welfare of society.

Here it is true that the appeal is still to abstract justice, but it is not an appeal to abstract justice only. In order to condemn interest on any such ground as this, it is necessary to assume or prove that to make interest illegal, or to confiscate it by taxation when it arises, or by any other means to render its enjoyment impossible, will as a matter of fact have the result desired-- namely, a permanent rise in the general level of prosperity. It is only by means of an assumption of this purely practical kind that the abstract moral principle can be applied to the case at all; and thus let us approach the problem from whatever side we will, we are brought from the region of theory down into that of practice, not, indeed, by an abrupt leap, but by a gradual and necessary transition. We are not abandoning our considerations of what, in abstract justice, ought to be; but we are compelled to interpret what ought to be by considerations of what, as the result of such and such arrangements, will be.

To sum up, then, the conclusions which we have reached thus far--if we confine our attention to those recipients of interest who have themselves produced the capital from which the interest is derived, and compare such incomes with those which renew themselves only as the result of continued effort, it is absolutely impossible, on any general theory of justice, to sanction the latter as earned, and condemn the former as unearned. If, on the other hand, we turn to those whose incomes consist of interest on capital produced by, and inherited from, their fathers, and if we argue that here at all events we come to a class of interest on which its living recipients can have no justifiable claim, since we start with admitting that it originates in the efforts of the dead, our argument, though plausible in its premises, is stultified by its logical consequence; since the same principle on which we are urged as a sacred duty to take the income in question away from its present possessors, would forbid our allowing it to pass into the possession of anybody else. In short, if continued daily labour, or else the exercise of invention, or some other form of ability, at some period of their lives by persons actually living, constitutes in justice the sole right to possession, the human race as a whole has no right to profit by any productive effort on the part of past generations; but each generation ought, so far as is practicable, to start afresh in the position of naked savages. The fact that nobody would maintain a fantastic proposition like this is sufficient to show that, on the tacit admission of everybody, it is impossible to attack interest by insisting on any abstract distinction between incomes that are earned and unearned, and treating the latter as felonious, while holding the former sacred. It is equally true, however, that on such grounds alone it is no less impossible to defend interest than to attack it; and here we arrive at what is the real truth of the matter--namely, that in cases like the present the principles of ideal justice do not, indeed, give us false guidance, but give us no guidance at all, unless we take them in connection with the concrete facts of society, and estimate social arrangements as being either right or wrong by reference to the practical consequences which do, or which would result from them.

The practical aspects of the question we will discuss in the following chapter.

CHAPTER XIV

THE SOCIALISTIC ATTACK ON INTEREST AND THE NATURE OF ITS SEVERAL ERRORS

If we reconsider what we have seen in the last chapter, we shall realise that the moral or theoretical attack on interest, as income which is unjustifiable because it has not been personally earned, is, when tested by the logic of those who make it, an attack, not on interest itself, but on bequest; and that such is the case will become even more evident when we see what the theory comes to, as translated into a practical programme.

The majority of those who attack interest to-day, no matter whether in other respects they are advocates of socialism or opponents of it, agree in declaring that what a man has personally produced he has a perfect right to enjoy and spend as he pleases. The only right they deny to him is the right to any further products which, before the capital has been spent by him, may result from the productive use of it. Now, the practical object with which this restriction is advocated is to render impossible, not accumulations of wealth (for these are recognised as legitimate when the reward of personal talent), but merely their perpetuation in the hands of others who are economically idle. So far, therefore, as this practical object is concerned, it would matter little whether the man by whom the accumulation was made were allowed to receive interest on it during his own lifetime or no, provided that this right to interest were not transmissible to his heir; or even whether he were allowed or were not allowed to leave anything to an heir at all. For the heir at best would merely receive a sum which, since it could not be used by him so as to bring about its own renewal, would be bound soon to exhaust itself; and the general effect of permitting bequests of this sterilised kind would differ from the effect of prohibiting bequests altogether, not because it would tend to render accumulated fortunes permanent, but only because it would protract for a decade or two the process of their inevitable dissipation.

We may, therefore, say that, for the purposes of the present discussion, the modern attack on interest, considered apart from any otherwise socialistic programme, practically translates itself into this--namely, the advocacy of a scheme which, as regards the actual producers of capital, leaves their existing rights both to principal and interest untouched, and would not even extinguish altogether their existing powers of bequest, but would limit the exercise of these to the principal sum only,[23] and prohibit the transmission to any private person of any right whatever to the usufruct of its productive employment.

Here, then, at last, we have something definite to discuss--a single proposed alteration in certain existing arrangements; and by comparing the situation which actually exists to-day with that which the proposed alteration, if carried into effect, would produce, we shall see whether the alteration is workable and practically defensible or no. Let us begin with the situation which actually exists to-day, confining ourselves to those features of it which are vital to the present issue.

Let us take two men of practically contrasted types, each of whom has inherited a capital of fifty thousand pounds. The ultimate object of each is, in one way or another, to make his capital provide him with the life that he most desires; but the first man is thoughtful, far-seeing, and shrewd, while the second cares for nothing but the gaiety and pleasure of the moment; and they deal with their capitals in accordance with their respective characters. The first meets, let us say, with the inventor of an agricultural machine, which will, if successfully manufactured, double the wheat crop of every acre to the cultivation of which it is applied. He places his capital, as a loan, in this inventor's hands. The machine is constructed, and used with the results desired; and the man who has lent the capital receives each year a proportion of the new loaves which are due to the machine's efficiency, and would not have existed otherwise. The second man invests his fortune in any kind of security which has the advantage of being turned easily into cash, and draws out month by month so many hundred pounds, without reference to anything but the pleasures he desires to purchase; and by the end of a few years both his capital and his income have disappeared.

Now, any one judging these men by the current standards of common-sense would, while praising the first as a model of moral prudence, condemn the second as a fool who had brought his ruin upon himself, and curtly dismiss him, if a bachelor, as being nobody's enemy but his own. But before we indorse either of these judgments as adequate, let us consider more minutely what in each case has been really done.

Let us start, then, with noting this. Whether a man invests his capital in any productive machine and then lives on the interest, or else spends it as income on his own personal pleasures, he is doing in one respect precisely the same thing. He is giving something to other men in order that they in return may make certain efforts for his benefit, of a kind which he himself prescribes. This is obviously true when, spending his capital as income, what he pays for is personal service, such as that of a butler or footman who polishes his silver plate. It is equally true when he pays for the plate itself. He is paying the silversmith so to exert his muscles that an ounce or a pound of silver may be wrought into a specific form. If he pays a toy-maker to make him a dancing-doll, he is virtually paying him to dance in his own person. He is paying him to go through a series of prescribed muscular movements. Similarly when he pays a large number of men to construct a productive machine instead of a doll or an ornament, he is paying for the muscular movements from which the machine results. Here we come back to one of the main economic truths to the elucidation of which our earlier chapters were devoted. It was there pointed out that the machinery of the modern world owes its existence to the fact that men of exceptional talent, by possessing the control of goods which a number of other men require, are able in return for the goods to make these other men exert themselves in a variety of minutely prescribed and elaborately co-ordinated ways. In short, all spending is, on the part of those who spend, a determination of the efforts of others in such ways as the spender pleases. Further, as was pointed out in an earlier chapter also, the only goods thus generally exchangeable for effort are those common necessaries of existence for which most men must always work, and which may here be represented by food, the first and the most important of them. Hence, whenever the question arises of how any given capital shall be treated--of whether it shall be invested or else spent as income--this capital must be regarded as existing in the indeterminate form of food, which is equally capable of being treated in one way or the other. And any man's capital represents for him, according to its amount, the power of feeding, and so determining the actions of a definite number of other men for some definite period. Since, therefore, the two capitalists whose conduct we have been taking as an illustration have been supposed by us to possess fifty thousand pounds apiece, we shall give precision to the situation if we say that each, at starting, has the power of feeding, and so determining the actions of, two hundred other men for a period of two years.

So much, then, being settled, let us consider these further facts. Both the capitalists, as we set out with observing, have in employing their capital the same ultimate object--namely, that of securing through the purchased efforts of others a continuous supply of things which will render their lives agreeable. And now in connection with this fact let us go back to another, which has also been pointed out before, that all efforts, the sole object of which is to please from moment to moment the man who directs and pays for them, are, whether embodied in the form of commodities or no, really reducible to some kind of personal service, if a toy-maker, in return for food, makes a dancing-doll for another man, he might just as well have pirouetted for so many hours himself; and if the purchaser would be more amused by a man's antics than by a puppet's, this is precisely what the toy-maker would have been set to do. In short, if we consider only the economic side of the matter, without reference to the moral, whenever a man spends anything on his own personal pleasure, he is virtually paying some other man, or a number of other men to dance for him.[24] What, therefore, both our capitalists desire as their ultimate object, is to keep as many men as they are able to provide with food always dancing for their pleasure, or in readiness to do so when wanted; but in setting themselves to achieve this object in their two different ways, what happens is as follows.

Both use their capital by dispensing it in the form of daily rations to two hundred other men, on condition that these men do something; but the first feeds the other men, not on condition that they dance for him, or do anything that ministers to his own immediate pleasure, but on condition that they construct a machine which will enable, as soon as it is finished, a given amount of human effort to double the amount of food which such effort would have produced otherwise. Thus, by the end of two years--the time which we suppose to be required for the machine's completion--though the original food-supply of the capitalist will all have been taken up and disappeared, its place will have been taken by a machine which will enable forever afterwards one-half of the two hundred men to produce food for the whole. A hundred men, therefore, are left for whom food can be permanently provided, without any effort to produce it being made by these men themselves; and since of this annual surplus a part--let us call it half--will be taken as interest on the machine by the man with whose capital it was constructed, he will now have the means of making fifty men dance for his pleasure in perpetuity; for as often as they have eaten up one supply of food, this, through the agency of the machine, will have been replaced by another.

Our second capitalist, meanwhile, who deals with his capital as income, starts with setting the dancers to dance for his behoof at once; and he keeps the whole two hundred dancing and doing nothing else, so long as he has food with which to feed them. This life is charming so long as it lasts, but in two years' time it abruptly comes to an end. The capitalist's cupboard is bare. He has no means of refilling it. The dancers will dance no more for him, for he cannot keep them alive; and the efforts for two years of two hundred men, as directed by a man who treats his capital as income, will now have resulted in nothing but the destruction of that capital itself, and a memory of muscular movements which, so far as the future is concerned, might just as well have been those of monkeys before the deluge.

Now, if we take the careers of our two capitalists as standing for the careers of two individuals only, and estimate them only as related to these men themselves, we might content ourselves with indorsing the judgment which conventional critics would pass on them, and say of the one that he had acted as his own best friend, and dismiss the other as nobody's enemy but his own. But we are, in our present inquiry, only concerned with individuals as illustrating kinds of conduct which are, or which might be, general; and the effects of their conduct, which we here desire to estimate, are its effects of it, not on themselves, but on society taken as a whole. If we look at the matter in this comprehensive way, we shall find that the facile judgments to which we have just alluded leave the deeper elements of our problem altogether untouched.

The difference between the ultimate results of the two ways of treating capital will, to the conventional critic, seem to have been sufficiently explained, by saying that the energy stored up in a given accumulation of food reappears when employed in one way, in the efficiency of a permanent machine; and is, when employed in the other, so far as human purposes are concerned, as completely lost as it would have been had it never existed. But if we reconsider a fact which was dwelt upon in our last chapter, we shall see that the difference is really much greater than this.

When the potential energy residing in so much food has been converted into the energy of so much human labour, and when this is so directed that a productive machine results from it, there is in the machine, as Dr. Crozier puts it, an indefinitely larger amount of "pure economic power," than that which has been expended in the work of the labourers' muscles. While the energy of the labourers has merely resulted in a bottle, or a cage, we may say, of sufficient strength, the genius of the man who directed them has captured and imprisoned an elemental slave in it, who, so long as the cage confines him, will supplement the efforts of human muscle with his own. But when the energy latent in food is converted into such efforts as dancing, the result produced is the equivalent of the human effort only. Thus in the modern world of scientific enterprise and invention, to invest capital in machinery and then live on the interest from it, means to press into the service of mankind an indefinite number of non-human auxiliaries, and year by year to live on a part of the products which these deathless captives are never tired of producing.

To spend capital as income on securing immediate pleasures means either to forgo the chance of adding any new auxiliaries to those that we possess already, or else to let those who are at our service already, one after one, escape us--or, in other words, to make the productive force now at the disposal of any prosperous modern country decline towards that zero of efficiency from which industrial progress starts, and which marks off helpless savagery from the first beginnings of civilisation.

It is no doubt inconceivable, in the case of any modern nation, that a climax of the kind just indicated could never reach its completion. If all the capitalists, for example, of Great Britain or America, were suddenly determined to live on their capital itself, they could do so only by continuing for a considerable time to employ a great deal of it precisely as it is employed at present. Indeed, so long as they continued to demand the luxuries which machines produce, it might seem that it was hardly possible for them to get rid of their capital at all. But what would really happen may be briefly explained thus:--

If we take the case of any modern country, the amount of its income at any given time depends for its sustentation on machines already in existence; and its increase is dependent on the gradual supersession of these by new ones yet more efficient. But the efficiency of the former would soon begin to decrease, and would ultimately disappear altogether, unless they were constantly repaired and their lost substance was renewed; while the latter would never exist unless there were men to make them. Hence, under modern conditions, in any prosperous and progressive country, a large portion of what is called the manufacturing class is always engaged, not in producing articles of consumption, comfort, or luxury, but in repairing and renewing the machines by which such articles are at present multiplied, or else in constructing new machines which shall supplement or replace the old. Thus, in Great Britain, towards the close of the nineteenth century, these makers and repairers of machinery were, with the exception of coal-miners, the industrial body whose proportional increase was greatest. In the modern world the spending of capital as income is a process which, in proportion as it became general, would accomplish itself by affecting the position of men like these. It would consist of a withdrawal of men who are at present occupied in maintaining existing machines, or else in constructing new ones from their anvils, hammers, files, lathes, and furnaces, and making them dance instead. This withdrawal would, in proportion as it became general, render the construction of new machines impossible, and would leave the efficiency of those now in use to exhaust itself.

That such is the case is illustrated on a small scale by the conduct of individuals who live on their capital now. If a farmer, whose capital consists largely of an agricultural plant, desires to spend more than his proceeds of his farm are worth, he virtually takes the men who have been mending his barns and reapers, and sets them to build a buggy which will take him to the neighbouring races. The varnish on the buggy is bought with the rust on the reaper's blades; the smart, weather-proof apron with the barn's unmended roof. If the managing body of a railroad pays a higher dividend to the shareholders than can be got out of its net earnings, the results are presently seen in cars that are growing dirty, in engines that break down, in rotten sleepers, and in trains that run off the track. The men who were once fed out of a certain portion of the traffic receipts to keep these things in repair, are now fed to dance for the shareholders, thus supplying them with spurious dividends. A farm or a railroad which was managed on these principles would ultimately cease to produce or to do anything for anybody; and if all modern capital were managed in a similar way, all the multiplied luxuries distinctive of modern civilisation would, one by one, disappear like crops which were left to rot for lack of machines to reap them with, and train services which had ceased because the engines were all burned out.

That such a climax should ever, in any modern country, complete itself cannot, let me say once more, be apprehended as a practical possibility; but it is practically impossible only because the earlier stages of the approach to it would lead to a situation that was intolerable long before it ceased to be irreparable. And here we reach the point to which the foregoing examination has been leading us. It is precisely this course of conduct, the end of which would be general ruin, that any attack on interest, by means of special taxation or otherwise, would, so long as it lasted, stimulate and render inevitable. Let me point out--though it ought in a general way to be self-evident--precisely how this is.

We start with assuming--for, as we have seen already, so much is conceded by those who attack interest to-day--that the owners of capital, however their rights may be restricted, still have rights to it of some kind. But a man's rights to his capital will not be rights at all unless they empower him to use it in one way or another as a means of ministering to his own personal desires; and it is possible for him so to use it in one or other of two ways only--either by keeping it in the form of some productive machine or plant, and living on a part of the values which this produces, or by trenching on the substance of the machine or the plant itself in the manner, and with the results, which have just been explained and analysed. If, therefore, capitalists are to be virtually deprived of their interest, either by means of a special tax on "unearned incomes" or otherwise, but are yet permitted to enjoy their capital somehow, no course is open to them but to employ for their private pleasures the men by whom this capital, in such forms as machines or railroads, is at present maintained, renewed, and kept from lapsing into a state in which it would be unable to do or to produce anything. And if any one still thinks that, by such a course of conduct, if ever it became general, as it would do under these conditions, the owners of capital would be injuring themselves alone, he need only reflect a little longer on one of our suggested illustrations, and ask himself whether the gradual deterioration of railroads would have no effect on the world beyond that of impoverishing the shareholders. It would obviously affect the many as much as it affected the few, and the kind of catastrophe that would result from the deterioration of railroads is typical of that which would result from the deterioration of capital generally.

It would, then, be a sufficient answer to those who attack interest, and propose to transfer it from its present recipients to the state, to elucidate, as has here been done, the two following points: firstly, that to interest as a means of enjoying wealth--the right to such enjoyment itself not being here disputed--the only alternative is a system which would thus prove fatal to everybody; and, further, that, conversely, the enjoyment of wealth through interest not only possesses this negative advantage, but is actively implicated in, and is the natural corollary of, that progressive accumulation of force in the form of productive machinery to which all the augmented wealth of the modern world is due. By the identification of the enjoyment of capital with the enjoyment of some portion of the products of it, the good of the individual capitalist is identified with the good of the community; for it will, in that case, be the object of all capitalists to raise the productivity of all capital to a maximum; while a system which would compel the possessor, if he is to enjoy his capital at all, to do so by diminishing its substance and allowing its powers to dwindle, would identify the only advantage he could possibly get for himself with the impoverishment of everybody else, and ultimately of himself also.

But the crucial facts of the case have not been exhausted yet. There are few phenomena of any complex society which are not traceable to more causes than one, or at least to one cause which presents itself under different aspects. Such is the case with interest. Its origin, its functions, and its justification, in the modern world, must be considered under an aspect, at which hitherto we have only glanced.

Throughout the present discussion we have been assuming that the questions at issue turn ultimately on the character of human motive. On both sides it has been assumed that men of exceptional powers will not produce exceptional amounts of wealth, unless they are allowed the right of enjoying some substantial proportion of it. This is a psychological truth which, together with its social consequences, has been dealt with elaborately in two of our earlier chapters. It was there shown that the production of exceptional wealth by those men whose peculiar powers alone enable them to produce it, involves efforts on their part which, unlike labour, cannot be exacted of them by any outside compulsion, but can only be educed by the prospect of a secured reward; and that this reward consists, as has just been said, of the enjoyment of a part of the product proportionate to the magnitude of the whole. But what the proportion should be, and in what manner it should be enjoyed, were questions which were then passed over. They were passed over in order that they might be discussed separately. It was pointed out, however, that the reward, in order to be operative, must be such as will be felt to be sufficient by these men themselves, and that its precise amount and quality can be determined by them alone--just as, if what we desire is to coax an invalid to eat, we can coax him only with food which he himself finds appetising. Let us now take these questions up again, and examine them more minutely, and we shall find that interest is justified from a practical point of view by the fact that the enjoyment of capital by this particular means is not only the sole manner of enjoying it which is consistent with the general welfare, but also constitutes the advantage which, in the eyes of most great producers, gives to capital the larger part of its value, and renders the desire of producing it efficient as a social motive.

The reasons why the right to interest forms, in the eyes of the active producers of capital, the main object of their activity are to be found, firstly, in the facts of family affection, and, secondarily, in those of general social intercourse, which together form the medium of by far the larger part of our satisfactions. In spite of the selfishness which distinguishes so much of human action, a man's desire to secure for his family such wealth as he can is one of the strongest motives of human activity known; and the fact that it operates in the case of many who are notoriously selfish otherwise, shows how deeply it is ingrained in the human character. One of the first uses to which a man who has produced great wealth puts it is in most cases to build a house more or less proportionate to his means; and it is his pride and pleasure to see his wife and children acclimatise themselves to their new environment. But such a house would lose most of its charm and meaning for him if the fortune which enabled him to live in it were to dwindle with each day's expenditure, and his family after his death were to be turned into the street, beggars. If each individual were a unit whose interests ended with himself; if generations were like stratified rocks, superposed one on another but not interconnected; if--to quote a pithy phrase, I do not know from whom--"if all men were born orphans and died bachelors," then the right to draw income from the products of permanently productive capital would for most men lose much of what now makes it desirable.

But since individuals and generations are not thus separated actually, but are, on the contrary, not merely as a scientific fact, but as a fact which is vivid to every one within the limits of his daily consciousness dovetailed into one another, and could not exist otherwise, a man's own fortune, with the kind of life that is dependent on it, is similarly dovetailed into fortunes of other people, and his present and theirs is dovetailed into a general future.

We have seen how this is the case with regard to his own family; but the matter does not end there. Individual households do not live in isolation; and there are for this fact two closely allied reasons. If they did there could be no marriage; there could also be nothing like social intercourse. It is social intercourse of a more or less extended kind that alone makes possible, not only love and marriage, but most of the pleasures that give colour to life. We see this in all ranks and in all stages of civilisation. Savages meet together in numerous groups to dance, like civilised men and women in New York or in London. The feast, or the meal eaten by a large gathering, is one of the most universal of all human enjoyments. But in all such cases the enjoyment involves one thing--namely, a certain similarity, underlying individual differences, between those persons who take part in it. Intimate social intercourse is, as a rule, possible only between those who are similar in their tastes and ideas with regard to the minute details which for most of us make up the tesser?of life's daily mosaic--similar in their manners, in their standards of beauty and comfort, in their memories, their prospects, or (to be brief) in what we may call their class habituations. This is true of all men, be their social position what it may. It is true, of course, that the quality of a man's life, as a whole, depends on other things also, of a wider kind than these. It depends not only on the fact, but also on his consciousness of the fact, that he is a citizen of a certain state or country, though with most of its inhabitants he will never exchange a word; or that he is a member of a certain church; or that, being a man and not a monkey, his destiny is identified with that of the human species. But, so far as his enjoyment of private wealth is concerned, each man as a rule, though to this there are individual exceptions, enjoys it mainly through the life of his own de facto class--the people whose manners and habits are more or less similar to his own, because they result from the possession of more or less similar means. He is, therefore, not interested in the permanence of his own wealth only. He is equally interested in the permanence of the wealth of a body of men, the life of which must, like that of all corporations, be continuous.

There is in this fact much more than at first appears. Let us go back to a point insisted on in the previous chapter. It was there shown, in connection with the question of abstract justice, that those who attack interest on the ground that it is essentially income for which its recipients give nothing in return, fall into the error of ignoring the element of time, without reference to which the whole process of life is unintelligible. It was shown, by various examples, that in a large number of cases the efforts which ultimately result in the production of great wealth do not produce it till after, often till long after, the original effort has come altogether to an end. Let us now take this point in connection, not with abstract theories, but with the concrete facts of conduct. Here again those who attack interest fall into the same error. For example, in answer to arguments used by me when speaking in America, one socialistic critic eagerly following another called my attention by name to persons notoriously wealthy, some of whom had never engaged in active business at all, while others had ceased to do so for many years; and demanded of me whether I contended that idlers such as these are doing anything whatever to produce the incomes which they are now enjoying. If they are, said the critics, let this wonderful fact be demonstrated. If they are not, then it must stand to reason that the community will gain, and cannot possibly suffer, by gradually taking the incomes of these persons away from them, and rendering it impossible that incomes of a similar kind shall in the future be ever enjoyed by anybody.

The general nature of the error involved in this class of argument can be shown by a very simple illustration. In many countries the government year by year makes a large sum by state lotteries. This may be a vicious procedure, but let us assume for the moment that it is legitimate, and that everybody is interested in its perpetuation. The largest of the prizes drawn in such lotteries is considerable--often amounting to more than twenty thousand pounds. Now, as soon as the drawing on any one occasion had been accomplished, it might be argued with perfect truth, in respect of that occasion only, that, the man who had won such fortune having done nothing to produce it, the community would be so much richer if the government, having paid the money to him, were to take it all back again by a special tax on winnings. This would be true with respect to that one occasion; but if any government were to follow such a procedure systematically, no one would ever buy a lottery ticket again, and the whole lottery system would thenceforth come to an end.

What is true of wealth won in lotteries is true of wealth in general. If the desire of possessing wealth is in any way a stimulus to the production of it, those who are motived to produce it by this desire to-day are motived by the desire of a something which they see to be desirable and attainable because they see it around them, embodied in the position of others, as the final result of the efforts of a long-past yesterday. If this result were never to be seen realised, no human being would make any effort to achieve it.

Let us--to go into particulars--suppose that the sole desire which moves exceptional men to devote their capacities to the augmentation of their country's wealth is the desire to join a class which, whether idle or active otherwise--whether devoted to mere pleasure or to philanthropy, or an enlightened patronage of the arts, or to speculative thought and study--is itself in an economic sense altogether unproductive. In order to join such a class, and to work with a view of joining it, society must be so organised that such a class can exist; and the fact of its existence constitutes the main moral magnet which, on our present hypotheses, is permanently essential to the development of the highest economic activity. Such being the case, then, the following conclusion reveals itself, which, although it may seem paradoxical, will be found on reflection to be self-evident--the conclusion namely, that a class which, if considered by itself, is absolutely non-productive, may, when taken in connection with the social system as a whole, be an essential and cardinal factor in the working machinery of production, constituting, as it would do by the mere fact of its existence, the charged electric accumulator by which the machinery is kept in motion; just as the mere existence of men, seen to be secure in their possession of the prizes of past lotteries, is the magnet which alone can make other men buy tickets for the lotteries of the future.

I have given this case as an assumption; but it is not an assumption only. The desire for wealth as a means of living in absolute idleness is probably confined, as a fact, in all countries to a few. In America especially it is a matter for surprise to strangers that men who have made fortune beyond the possibilities of pleasurable expenditure so rarely retire on them to cultivate the pursuits of leisure. But even in America, if they do not value leisure for themselves, they value it for their women, to whom, there as in all countries, four-fifths of the charm and excitement of private life are due; and the sustained possibility of leisure, even if not the enjoyment of it--a possibility which can rest only on a basis of sustained fortunes--is the main advantage which, in all civilised countries, gives wealth its meaning for those who already possess it, and its charm for those who are, in order to possess it, exerting at any given moment their energies and their intellect in producing it.

The source of such sustained fortunes, in their distinctively modern form, is, as we have seen already, such and such forces of nature, which, captured and embodied in machines and other appliances by the masters of science and men of executive energy, and subsequently directed by other men of cognate talents, supplement the efficiency of ordinary human labour, thus yielding the surplus of which modern fortunes are a part, the remainder forming a fund which diffuses itself throughout the mass of the community. That part of the surplus which constitutes such fortunes is interest; and now let us sum up what in this and the previous chapter our examination of the criticisms directed against interest has shown us.

In the first place, then, we saw that the theoretical attack on interest, on the ground that it is income which is not earned by the recipients, but is virtually taken by the few from the products of the labour of the many, is chimerical in its moral and false in its economic implications.

We saw, in the second place, coming down to the practical aspects of the question, that interest is the only form in which the owners of capital can enjoy their wealth at all, without drying up the sources from which most modern wealth springs, thus bringing ruin to the community no less than to themselves.

We saw, in the third place, that, quite apart from the welfare of the community, interest constitutes, for the owners of wealth themselves, the means of enjoying it which mainly makes it desirable, and the object for the sake of which, at any given moment, the master spirits of industry are engaged in producing and increasing it.

The reader must observe, however, that this conclusion is here stated in general terms only. It has not been contended--for this question has not been touched upon--that interest may not, when received in certain amounts, be justifiably made the subject of some special taxation. Any such question must be decided by reference to special circumstances, and cannot be discussed apart from them. Nor has it been contended that, within certain limits, the power of bequest is not susceptible of modification without impairing the energies of the few or the general prosperity of the many. The sole point insisted on here is this: that any special tax on interest, or any tampering with the powers of bequest, begins to be disastrous to all classes alike, if it renders, and in proportion as it renders to any appreciable degree, the natural rewards of the great producers of wealth less desirable in their own eyes than they are and otherwise would be.

FOOTNOTES:

[23] Mr. G. Wilshire, in his detailed criticism of my American speeches, states twice over the modern socialistic doctrine as to this point. The maker or inheritor of capital, he says, could, under socialism, "buy all the automobiles he wanted, all the diamonds, all the champagne; or he could build a palace. In other words, he could spend his income in consumable goods, but he could not invest either in productive machinery or in land."

[24] This is merely saying that all economic effort has, for its ultimate aim, a desirable state of consciousness, which might be contemptible if it really depended on looking on at dances, or refined if it depended on the cultivation of flowers, or listening to great singers, or witnessing the performance of great plays, or on the enlargement of the mind by travel.

CHAPTER XV

EQUALITY OF OPPORTUNITY

Having now dealt with two of those three ideas or conceptions which, though not necessarily connected with the specific doctrines of socialism, owe much of their present diffusion to the activity of socialistic preachers-- that is to say, the idea, purely statistical, that labour, as contrasted with the directive ability of it, actually produces much more than it gets, and the further idea that the many could ameliorate their own position by appropriating the interest now received by the few; having dealt with these two ideas, it remains for us to consider the third--namely, that which is generally suggested by the formula Equality of Opportunity, or, more particularly (for this is what concerns us here), equality of opportunity in the domain of economic production.

We must start with recollecting that if the wealth of a country depends mainly, as we have here seen that it does, on the efforts of those of its citizens whose industrial talent is the greatest, the more effectively all such talent is provided with an opportunity of exerting itself the greater will the wealth and prosperity of that country be. In other words, if potential talent is to be actualised, opportunity is as needful for its exercise as is the stimulus of a proportionate reward. That economic opportunity ought, therefore, to be equalised, so far as possible, is, as an abstract principle, too obvious to need demonstration. But abstract principles are useless till we apply them to a concrete world; and when we apply our abstract doctrine of opportunity to the complex facts of society and human nature, a principle so simple in theory will undergo as many modifications as a film of level water will if we spill it over an uneven surface.

The first fact which will confront us, when we come down from theory to facts, is one which could not be more forcibly emphasised than it has been by a socialistic writer,[25] whose utterances were quoted in one of our previous chapters. This is the fact that, in respect of their powers of production, just as of most others, human beings are in the highest degree unequal. They are unequal in intellect and imagination. More especially they are unequal in energy, alertness, executive capacity, initiative and in what we may describe generally as practical driving force. Such being the case, then, if it could actually be brought about that every individual at a given period of his life should start with economic opportunities identical with those of his contemporaries, each generation would be like horses chosen at haphazard, and started at the same instant to struggle over the same course in the direction of a common winning-post. And what would be the result? A few individuals would be out of sight in a moment; the mass at various distances would be struggling far behind them, and a large residuum would have been blown before it had advanced a furlong. Thus, by making men's adventitious opportunities equal, we should no more equalise the result for the sake of which the opportunities were demanded than we should give every cab-horse in London a chance of winning the Derby by allowing it on Derby Day to go plodding over the course at Epsom. On the contrary, by inducing all to contemplate the same kind of success, we should be multiplying the sense of failure and dooming the majority to a gratuitous discontent with positions in which they might have taken a pride had they not learned to look beyond them.

And now, from this fact, to which we shall come back presently, let us turn to the question of how, and in what respects, equality of opportunity is in practical life attainable.

The most obvious manner in which an approach to such equality can be made is by an equalisation of opportunities for education in early life, or, in other words, by a similar course of schooling, a similar access to books, and similar leisure for studying them. But even here, at this preliminary stage, we shall find that the equality of opportunity is to a large extent illusory. Let us suppose that there are two boys, equal in general intelligence, and unequal only in their powers of mental concentration, who start their study of German side by side in the same class-room. One boy, in the course of a year or so, will be able to read German books almost as easily as books in his own language, while the other will hardly be able to guess the drift of a sentence without laborious reference to his hated grammar and dictionary. Now, when once a situation such as this has arisen, the opportunities of the two boys have ceased to be equal any longer. The one has placed himself at an indefinite advantage over the other, which is quite distinct from the superiority originally inherent in himself. Among the educational opportunities which reformers desire to equalise, one of the chief is that of access to adequate libraries; and it is, they say, in this respect more perhaps than any other that the rich man has at present an unfair advantage over the poor. It is virtually this precise advantage that will now be in possession of the boy who has thus far outstripped his classmate. In his mastery of German he has a key to a vast literature--a key which the other has not. He is now like a rich man with an illimitable library of his own, while the other by comparison is like a poor man who can get at no books at all. Thus if opportunity, in its most fundamental form, were equalised for all boys, no matter how completely, the equality would be only momentary. It would begin to disappear by the end of the first few months, not because the boys would still, as they did at starting, be bringing to their tasks intrinsically unequal faculties, but because some of them would have already monopolised the aid of an adventitious knowledge by which the practical efficiency of their natural faculties would be multiplied.

But education is merely a preliminary to the actual business of life. Let us pass on to the case of our equally educated youths when they enter on the practical business of making their own fortunes. What kind of equal opportunity can be possibly provided for them now?

Since socialists are the reformers who, in dealing with objects aimed at, are least apt to be daunted by practical difficulties, let us see how equality of opportunity in business life is conceived of and described by them. The general contention of socialists in this respect is, says one of their best-known American spokesmen,[26] "that the fact that capital is now in the hands of private persons gives them an unfair advantage over those who own nothing," for capital consists of the implements of advantageous production; and socialists, he says, would secure an equality of industrial opportunity for all by "vesting the ownership of the means of production in the state"; the result of which procedure would, he goes on, be this: "that every one would have his own canoe, and it would be up to each to do his own paddling."

Now, purists in thought and argument might make it a subject of complaint, perhaps, that the writer, as soon as he reaches a vital part of his argument, should lapse into the imagery of an old music-hall song. But such an objection would be very much misplaced, for the ideas entertained by socialists as to this particular point closely resemble those which make music-hall songs popular. They consist of familiar images which are accepted without being analysed; and the image of man seated in an industrial canoe of his own, and paddling it just as he pleases without reference to anybody else, very admirably represents the lot which socialists promise to everybody, and which dwells as a possibility in the imagination of even their serious thinkers. But let us take this dream in connection with facts of the modern world, which these men, in much of their reasoning, themselves recognise as unalterable, and we shall see it give place to realities of a very different aspect.

To judge from our author's language, one would suppose that modern capital was made up entirely of separate little implements like sewing-machines, and that every one would, if the state were the sole capitalist, receive on application a machine of the same grade, which he might take away with him, and use or break in a corner. Now, if modern capital were really of this nature, the state no doubt might conceivably do something like what the writer suggests, in the way of dealing out similar industrial opportunities to everybody. But, as he himself is perfectly well aware, the distinctive feature of capital in the modern world is one which renders any such course impossible. Modern capital, as a whole, in so far as it consists of implements, consists not of implements which can be used by each user separately. It consists of enormous mechanisms, with the works and structures pertaining to them, which severally require to be used by thousands of men at once, and which no one of the number can use without reference to the operations of the others. If the state were to acquire the ownership of all the steel-mills at Pittsburg, how could it do more than is done by their present owners, to confer on each of the employ 闤 any kind of position analogous to that of a man "who has his own canoe"? The state could just as easily perform the literal feat of cutting up the Lusitania into a hundred thousand dinghys, in each of which somebody would enjoy the equal opportunity of paddling a passenger from Sandy Hook to Southampton.

But we will not tie our author too closely to the terms of his own metaphor. The work from which I have just quoted is a booklet[27] in which he devoted himself to the task of refuting in detail the arguments urged by myself in the course of my American speeches. We will, therefore, turn to his criticism of what, in one of my speeches, I said about the state post-office, and we shall there get further light with regard to his real meaning. I asked how any sorter or letter-carrier employed in the post-office by the state was any more his own master, or had any more opportunities of freedom, than a messenger or other person employed by a private firm. Our author's answer is this: "That the public can determine what the wages of a postman shall be--that is, they can, if they so choose (by their votes), double the wages now prevailing." Therefore, our author proceeds, "the postal employ? in a manner, may be considered as a man employing himself." Now, first let me observe that, as was shown in our seventh chapter, wages under socialism, just as under the present system, could be no more than a share of the total product of the community; and the claims advanced to a share of this by any one group of workers would be consequently limited by the claims of all the others. The question, therefore, of whether the postmen's wages should be doubled at any time, or whether they might not have to be halved, would not depend only on votes, but, also and primarily, on the extent of the funds available; and in so far as it depended on votes at all, the votes would not be those of the postmen. They would be the votes of the general public, and any special demand on the part of one body of workers would be neutralised by similar demands on the part of all the others. Further, if these "employers of themselves" could not determine their own wages, still less would they determine the details of the work required of them. A postman, like a private messenger, is bound to do certain things, not one of which he prescribes personally to himself. At stated hours he must daily be present at an office, receive a bundle of letters, and then set out to deliver them at private doors, in accordance with orders which he finds written on the envelopes. Such is the case at present, and socialism would do nothing to modify it. If our author thinks that a man, under these conditions, is his own employer, our author must be easily satisfied, and we will not quarrel with his opinion. It will be enough to point out that the moment he descends to details his promise that socialism would equalise economic opportunity for all reduces itself to the contention that the ordinary labourer or worker would, if the state employed him, have a better chance of promotion and increased wages than he has to-day, when employed by a private firm, and (we may add, though our author does not here say so) that some sort of useful work would be devised by the state for everybody.

Now, although every item of this contention, and especially the last, is disputable, let us suppose, for argument's sake, that it is, on the whole, well founded. Even so, we have not touched the real crux of the question. We have dealt only with the case of the ordinary worker, who fulfils the ordinary functions which must always be those of nine men out of every ten, let society be constituted in what way we will. It remains for us to consider the case of those who are fitted, or believe themselves to be fitted, for work of a wider kind, and who aspire to gain, by performing this, an indefinitely ampler remuneration. This ambitious and exceptionally active class is the class for which the promise of equal opportunities possesses its main significance, and in its relation to which it mainly requires to be examined. Indeed, the writer from whom we are quoting recognises this himself; for he gives his special attention to the economic position of those who, in greater or less degree, are endowed with what he calls "genius"; and in order to illustrate how socialism would deal with these, he cites two cases from the annals of electrical engineering, in which opportunities, not forthcoming otherwise, were given by the state to inventors of realising successful inventions.

Now, what our author and others who reason like him forget, is that the opportunities with which we are here concerned differ in one all-important particular from those which concern us in the case either of education or of ordinary employment. If one boy uses his educational opportunities ill, he does nothing to prejudice the opportunities of others who use them well. Should a sorter of letters, who, if he had been sharp and trustworthy, might have risen to the highest and best-paid post in his department, throw his opportunities away by inattention or otherwise, the loss resulting is confined to the man himself. The opportunities open to his fellows remain what they were before. But when we come to industrial activity of those higher and rarer kinds, on which the sustained and progressive welfare of the entire community depends, such as invention, or any form of far-reaching and original enterprise, the kind of opportunity which a man requires is not an opportunity of exerting his own faculties in isolation, like a sorter who is specially expert in deciphering illegible addresses. It is an opportunity of directing the efforts of a large number of other men. Apart from the case of craftsmanship and artistic production, all the higher industrial efforts are reducible to a control of others, and can be made only by men who have the means of controlling them. Since this is one of the principal truths that have been elucidated in the present volume, it is sufficient to reassert it here, without further comment. If, therefore, a man is to be given the opportunity of embodying and trying an invention in a really practical form, it will be necessary to put at his disposal, let us disguise the fact as we may, the services of a number of other men who will work in accordance with his orders. This, as we have seen already, is what is done by the ordinary investor whenever he lends capital to an inventor. He supplies him with the food by which the requisite subordinates must be fed; and the state, were the state the capitalist, would do virtually the same thing. It could give him his opportunity in no other way.

Further, if the invention in question turns out to be successful--here is another point which has already been explained and emphasised--the wage-capital which has been consumed by the labourers is replaced by some productive implement, which is more than the equivalent of the labour force spent in constructing it. If, on the other hand, the invention turns out to be a failure, the wage-capital is wasted, and, so far as the general welfare is concerned, the state might just as well have thrown the whole of it into the sea. Since, then, the opportunities which the state would have at its disposal, would consist at any moment of a given amount of capital, and since any portion of this which was used unsuccessfully would be lost, the number of opportunities which the state could allocate to individuals would be limited, and each opportunity which was wasted by one man would diminish the number that could be placed at the disposal of others.

Now, any one who knows anything of human nature and actual life knows this--that the number of men who firmly and passionately believe in the value of their own inventions, or other industrial projects, is far in excess of those whose ideas and projects have actually any value whatsoever. When the Great Eastern, the largest ship of its time, had been built on the Thames by the celebrated engineer Brunel, its launching was attended with unforeseen and what seemed to be insuperable difficulties. Mr. Brunel's descendants have, I believe, still in their possession, a collection of drawings, sent him by a variety of inventors, and representing all sorts of devices by which the launching might be accomplished. All were, as the draughtsmanship was enough to show, the work of men of high technical training; but the practical suggestions embodied in one and all of them could not have been more grotesque had they emanated from a home for madmen. To have given an equality of opportunity to all this tribe of inventors of putting their devices to the test would have probably cost more than the building of the ship itself, and the ship at the end would have been stranded in the dock still. This curious case is representative, and is sufficiently illustrative of the fact that opportunity of this costly kind could be conceded to a few only of those who would demand, and believe themselves to deserve it; and the state, as the trustee of the public, would have, unless it were prepared to ruin the nation, to be incomparably more cautious than any private investor.[28]

Of the general doctrine, then, that the opportunities of all should be equal, we may repeat that, as an abstract proposition, it is one which could be contested by nobody; but we have seen that, when applied to societies of unequal men, and to the various tasks of life, its original simplicity is lost, and it does not become even intelligible until we divest it of a large part of its implications. Economic or industrial opportunity is, we have seen, of three kinds: firstly, educational opportunity; secondly, the opportunity of performing and receiving the full equivalent of an ordinary task or service, such as that of a postman, the value of which depends on its conformity to a prescribed pattern or schedule; and thirdly, opportunity of directing the work of others, thereby initiating new enterprises or realising new inventions--a kind of opportunity requiring the control of capital, which capital, whether provided by the state or otherwise, would be lost to the community unless it were used efficiently.

With regard to educational opportunity--it has been seen that it is possible to equalise this, approximately if not entirely, at a given time in the early lives of all, but that it would be possible to maintain the equality for a short time only.

With regard to opportunities of earning a livelihood subsequently by performing one or other of those ordinary and innumerable tasks which must always fall to the lot of four men out of every five, we may say that an equalisation of opportunities of this kind is the admitted object of every reformer and statesman who believes that the prosperity of a country is synonymous with the welfare of its inhabitants. In achieving this object there are, however, two difficulties--one being the difficulty, occasional and often frequent in any complex society, of devising work which has any practical value, and replaces its own cost, for all those who are able and willing to perform it; the other being the difficulty which arises from the existence of persons who are incapacitated, by some species of vice, from performing, or from performing adequately, any useful work whatever. We must here content ourselves with observing that the official directors of industry, who would constitute the state under socialism, would be no more competent to solve the first than are the private employers of to-day, while there is nothing in the scheme of society put forward by socialists, which even purports to supply any solution of the second, other than a more drastic application of the methods applied to-day.

Thirdly, with regard to equality of opportunity for those whose main ambition is not to be provided with some task-work performable by their own hand, but to achieve some position which will enable them to prescribe tasks to others, and thus do justice to their real or supposed talents by the construction of great machines, or the organisation of great enterprises--in other words, with regard to those persons whose ambition is to obtain what are called the prizes of life, and who think themselves treated unjustly if they find themselves unable to gain them--we have seen that to provide equal opportunities for all or even for most of these, is in the very nature of things impossible. The fundamental reason of this, let me say once more, is the fact that the number of men possessing sufficient talent to conceive ambitious schemes of one kind or another far exceeds the number of those whose talents are capable of producing any useful results; and to give to this majority opportunities of testing their projects by experiment would be merely to deplete the resources of the entire nation for the sake of demonstrating to one particular class that abortive talents are worse than no talents at all.

Here we are in the presence of a fact far wider than this special manifestation of it. In the animal and the vegetable world, no less than in the human, the successes of nature are the siftings of its partial failures; and in order to secure such services as are really productive it must always be necessary to squander opportunities to a certain extent in the testing of talents which ultimately turn out to be barren. But cases of this kind may, at all events, be reduced to a minimum; and the reduction of their number is possible, because they are largely an artificial product. In order to understand how this is, we must go back again to the question of equality of opportunity in education, and consider it under an aspect which has not yet engaged our attention.

We started with supposing the establishment of a system of education which would offer to all the same books and teachers, and also--for this was part of our assumption--equal leisure to profit by them; and we noted how soon opportunities would cease to be equal on account of the different uses which would be made of them by different students. What must now be noted is that as matters have been conducted hitherto, attempts to make educational opportunities equal do tend to produce an equality of a certain kind. Though they have no tendency to equalise powers of achievement, they tend to produce an artificial equality of expectation. In order to elucidate the nature of this fact, and its significance, I cannot do better than quote a passage from Ruskin, admirable for its trenchant felicity, which, since it occurs in a book much admired by socialists, may be commended to their special attention.[29] Economic demand, Ruskin says, is the expression of economic desires; but the constitution of human nature is such that these desires are divisible into two distinct kinds--desires for the commodities which men "need," and desires for commodities which they "wish for." The former arise from those appetites and appetencies in respect of which all are equal. They are virtually a fixed quantity, and the economic commodities requisite for their healthy satisfaction constitute a minimum which is virtually the same for all men. The latter, instead of being fixed, are capable of indefinite variation, and in these--the desires for what men "wish for" but do not "need"--we have the origin "of three-fourths of the demands existing in the world." "These demands are," he proceeds, "romantic. They are founded on visions, idealisms, hopes, and affections, and the regulation of the purse is, in its essence, regulation of the imagination and the heart."

With the demands which originate in men's equal needs we are not concerned here. It is impossible to modify them appreciably either by education or otherwise; but the desires or wishes which Ruskin so happily calls "romantic" vary in intensity and character to an almost indefinite degree, not only in different individuals, but also in the same individuals when submitted to different circumstances. Those of them, indeed, which are most generally felt are often, to speak strictly, not so much desires as fancies; and while the image of their fulfilment may please or amuse the imagination, their non-fulfilment produces no sense of want. So long as they are merely fancies, they raise no practical question. They raise a practical question only when their insistence is such that their non-fulfilment produces an active sense of privation; and whether in the case of any given individual they reach or do not reach this pitch of intensity depends upon two things. One of these is the individual's congenital temperament, his talents, his strength of will, and the vividness or vagueness of his imagination. Education, understood in its more general sense, is the other. Now, men varying as they do in respect of their congenital characters, the strength of their romantic wishes bears naturally some proportion to their own capacities for attempting to satisfy these wishes for themselves. Few men, for example, have naturally a strong wish for conditions which will enable them to exercise exceptional power, unless they are conscious of possessing exceptional powers to exercise. Hence, though this consciousness is in many cases deceptive, the struggle of men for power is confined within narrow limits, and the disappointments which embitter those who fail to attain it are naturally confined within narrow limits also. So long as matters stand thus, the majority of men are unaffected. But wishes which are naturally confined to exceptional men, who are more or less capable of realising them, are susceptible by education of indefinite extension to others who are not so qualified; and in the case of these last, the results which they produce are different. They multiply the number of those who demand preferential opportunities, in order that they may enter on a struggle in which they must ultimately fail.

They multiply the number of those, to a still greater extent, who demand that positions or possessions shall be somehow provided for them by society, without reference to any struggle on their own part at all. The artificial diffusion of "wish" among these two distinguishable classes is thus accomplished by education in somewhat different ways; but the modus operandi is in one respect the same in both. It consists of an artificial enlarging, in the case of all individuals alike, of the ideas entertained by them of their natural social rights; and an active craving is thus generalised for possessions and modes of life, which nine men out of ten would otherwise have never wasted a thought upon, and which not one out of ten can possibly make his own. How easily this idea of rights is susceptible of enlargement by teaching, and how efficient it is in creating a desire where none would have existed otherwise, is vividly illustrated by those not infrequent cases in which men, who for half their lives have considered themselves fortunate in the possession of moderate affluence, have suddenly been led to suppose themselves the heirs of peerages or great estates, and have died insane or bankrupt in consequence of their vain endeavours to secure rank or property which, had it not been for a purely adventitious idea, would have affected their hopes and wishes no more than the moon did. It is precisely in this manner that much of the education of to-day operates in consequence of current attempts to equalise it[30]; and since education is the cause of the evils here in question, it is in some reform of education that we must hope to find a cure. What the general nature of this reform would be can be indicated in a few words. It would not involve a reversal, it would involve a modification only, of the principle now in vogue, and can, indeed, best be expressed by means of the same formula, if we do but add to it a single qualifying word-- that is to say, the word "relative" prefixed to the word "equality," when we speak of equality of opportunity as the end at which we ought to aim. Let me explain my meaning.

The logical end of all action is happiness; and happiness, so far as it depends on economic conditions at all, is an equation between desire and attainment. The capacities of men being unequal, and the objects of desire which they could, under the most favourable circumstances, make their own, being unequal likewise, the ideal object of education, as a means to happiness, is twofold. It is, on the one hand, so to develop each man's congenital faculties as to raise them to their maximum power of providing him with what he desires; and on the other hand to limit his desires, by a due regulation of his expectations, to such objects as his faculties, when thus developed, render approximately if not completely attainable. Thus, relatively to the individual, the ideal object of education is in all cases the same; but since individuals are not equal to one another, education, if it is to perform an equal service for each, must be in its absolute character to an indefinite extent various; just as a tailor, if he is to give to all his customers equal opportunities of being well dressed, will not offer them coats of the same size and pattern. He will offer them coats which are equal only in this--namely, their equally successful adaptation to the figures of their respective wearers.

Of course, so to graduate any actual course of education that in the case of each individual it is the best which it is possible to conceive for him--that it should at once enable him to make the most of his powers, and "regulate," as Ruskin says, "his imagination and his hopes" in accordance with them, would require a clairvoyance and prevision not given to man; but the end here specified--namely, an equality of opportunity which is relative--is the only kind of equality which is even theoretically possible; and it is one, moreover, to which a constant approximation can be made. The absolute equality which is contemplated by socialists, and by others who are more or less vaguely influenced by socialistic sentiment, is, on the contrary, an ideal which either could not be realised at all, or which, in proportion as it was realised, would be ruinous to the nation which provided it, and would bring nothing but disappointment to those who were most importunate in demanding it. The only conceivable means, indeed, by which it could be extended beyond the first few years of life, would be by a constant process of handicapping--that is to say, by applying to education the same policy that trade-unions apply to ordinary labour. If one bricklayer has laid more bricks than his fellows, he virtually has to wait until the others have caught him up. Similarly, if equality of opportunity, other than an equality that is relative, were to be maintained in the sphere of education, a clever boy who had learned to speak German in a year would have to be coerced into idleness until every dunce among his classmates could speak it as well as he; and a similar process would be repeated in after-life. This policy, as has been pointed out already, is, even if wasteful, not ruinous in the sphere of ordinary labour--a fact which shows how wide the difference is between the ordinary faculties, as applied to industry, and the exceptional; but no one in his senses, not even the most ardent apostle of equality, would dream of recommending its application to efforts of a higher kind, and demand that the clever boys should periodically be made to wait for the stupid, or that the best doctor in the presence of a great pestilence should not be allowed to cure more patients than the worst one.

If, then, it is, as it must be, the ideal aim of social arrangements generally to enable each to raise his capacities to their practical maximum, and adjust his desires and his expectations to the practical possibilities of attainment, "relative equality of opportunity," firstly in education and secondly in practical life, is a formula which accurately expresses the means by which this end is to be secured; but the absolute equality which is contemplated by socialists and others is an ideal which, the moment we attempted to translate it into terms of the actual, would begin to fall to pieces, defeating its own purpose; and there is nothing in socialism, were socialism otherwise practicable, any more than there is the existing system, which would obviate this result.

Indeed, it may be observed further that, though the idea of equality of opportunity in general is not inconsistent with a socialistic scheme of society, as socialists of the more thoughtful kind have now come to conceive of it, it belongs distinctively to the domain of the fiercest individual competition. For in so far as socialism differs from ordinary individualism, it differs from it in this--that, instead of encouraging each man to do his utmost because what he gets will be proportionate to what he does, it aims at establishing a greater equality in what men get by making this independent of whether they do much or little; in which case the main concern of the individual would be the certainty of getting what he wanted, not the opportunity of producing it.

The three ideas or conceptions, then, which have engaged our attention in this and the three preceding chapters--namely, the idea that labour does, as a statistical fact, produce far more in values than it at present gets back in wages; the idea that the mass of the population could permanently augment its resources by confiscating all dividends as fast as they became due, and the idea that it is possible to provide for unequal men, for more than a moment of their lives, equal opportunities of experimenting with their real or imaginary powers, are ideas, indeed, which have all the vices characteristic of socialistic thought; but the first and the third have no necessary connection with socialism, and the second is not peculiar to it. We will now return to it as a system of exclusive and distinctive doctrines, and sum up, in general terms, the conclusions to which our examination of it is calculated to lead far-seeing and practical men, and more especially active politicians.

FOOTNOTES:

[25] The Christian Socialist author of _The Gospel for To-day_. See chapter on Christian Socialism.

[26] Mr. Wilshire, in his volume of criticism on my American speeches.

[27] _Socialism: the Mallock-Wilshire Argument._ By Gaylord Wilshire. New York, 1907.

[28] While this work was in the press, one of the English Labour members, Mr. Curran, at a public meeting, gave his views, as a socialist, about this very question--equality of industrial opportunity--and as an example of such opportunity already in existence, he mentioned the cash-credit system, which prevails in banks in Scotland. He seemed unaware that such advances of capital made in this system are made to picked men only. These men, moreover, have the strongest stimulus to effect in the face that they will keep all their profits. If a socialistic state gave cash-credits to everybody, it would confiscate all the profits if the workers were successful, and have no remedy against them if they failed.

[29] _Unto This Last._

[30] See note to previous chapter, referring to the recent Red Catechism for socialist Sunday schools, in which children are taught, as the primary article of faith, that the wage-earners produce everything, that the productivity of all is practically equal, and that all are entitled to expect precisely the same kind of life.

CHAPTER XVI

THE SOCIAL POLICY OF THE FUTURE

I was constantly asked by socialists in America whether I really believed that society, as it is, is perfect, and that there are no evils and defects in it which are crying aloud for remedy. Unless I believed this--and that I could do so was hardly credible--I ought, they said, if I endeavoured to discredit the remedy proposed by themselves, to suggest another, which would be better and equally general, of my own.

Now, such an objection, as it stands, I might dismiss by curtly observing that I did not, and could not, suggest any remedy other than socialism, partly because the purport of my entire argument was that socialism, if realised, would not be a remedy at all; and partly because, for the evils that afflict society, no general remedy of any kind is possible. The diseases of society are various, and of various origin, and there is no one drug in the pharmacopoeia of social reform which will cure or even touch them all, just as there is no one drug in the pharmacopoeia of doctors which will cure appendicitis, mumps, sea-sickness, and pneumonia indifferently--which will stop a hollow tooth and allay the pains of childbirth.

But though such an answer would be at once fair and sufficient, if we take the objection in the spirit in which my critics urged it, the objection has more significance than they themselves suspected, and it requires to be answered in a very different way. Socialism may be worthless as a scheme, but it is not meaningless as a symptom. Rousseau's theory of the origin of society, of the social contract, and of a cure for all social evils by a return to a state of nature, had, as we all know now, no more relation to fact than the dreams of an illiterate drunkard; but they were not without value as a vague and symbolical expression of certain evils from which the France of his day was suffering. As a child, I was told a story of an old woman in Devonshire who, describing what was apparently some form of dyspepsia, said that "her inside had been coming up for a fortnight," and still continued to do so, although during the last few days "she had swallowed a pint of shot in order to keep her liver down." The old woman's diagnosis of her own case was ridiculous; her treatment of it, if continued, would have killed her; but both were suggestive, as indications that something was really amiss. The reasoning of Rousseau, who contended that the evils of the modern world were due to a departure from primeval conditions which were perfect, and that a cure for them must be sought in a return to the manner of life which prevailed among the contemporaries of the mammoth, and the immediate descendants of the pithekanthropos, was identical in kind with the reasoning of the old woman. The reasoning of the socialists is identical in kind with both. It consists of a poisonous prescription founded on a false diagnosis. But just as the diagnosis, no matter how grotesque, which a patient makes of his or of her own sufferings, and even the remedies which his or her fancy suggests, often assist doctors to discover what the ailment really is, so does socialism, alike in its diagnosis and its proposed cure, call attention to the existence of ailments in the body politic, and may even afford some clue to the treatment which the case requires, though this will be widely different from what the sufferer fancies.

Such being the case, then, in order that a true treatment may be adopted, the first thing to be done is to show the corporate patient precisely how and why the socialistic diagnosis is erroneous, and the proposed socialistic remedies incomparably worse than the disease. To this preparatory work the present volume has been devoted. Let us reconsider the outline of its general argument. As thoughtful socialists to-day are themselves coming to admit, the augmented wealth distinctive of the modern world is produced and sustained by the ability of the few, not by the labour of the many. The ability of the few is thus productive in the modern world in a manner in which it never was productive in any previous period, because, whereas in earlier ages the strongest wills and the keenest practical intellects were devoted to military conquest and the necessities of military defence, they have, in the modern world, to a constantly increasing degree, been deflected from the pursuits of war and concentrated on those of industry. But the old principle remains in operation still, of which military leadership was only one special exemplification. Nations now grow rich through industry as they once grew rich through conquest, because new commanders, with a precision unknown on battle-fields, direct the minutest operations of armies of a new kind; and the only terms on which any modern nation can maintain its present productivity, or hope to increase it in the future, consist in the technical submission of the majority of men to the guidance of an exceptional minority. As for the majority--the mass of average workers--they produce to-day just as much as, and no more than, they would produce if the angel of some industrial Passover were henceforward to kill, each year on a particular day, every human being who had risen above the level of his fellows, and, in virtue of his knowledge, ingenuity, genius, energy, and initiative, was capable of directing his fellows better than they could direct themselves. If such an annual decimation were inaugurated to-morrow in civilised countries such as Great Britain and America, the mass of the population would soon sink into a poverty deeper and more helpless than that which was their lot before the ability of the few, operating through modern capital, began to lend to the many an efficiency not their own. In other words, the entire "surplus values"--to adopt the phrase of Marx--which have been produced during the last hundred and fifty years, have been produced by the ability of the few, and the ability of the few only;[31] and every advance in wages, and every addition to the general conveniences of life, which the labourers now enjoy, is a something over and above what they produce by their own exertions. It is a gift to the many from the few, or, at all events, it has its origin in the sustentation and the multiplication of their efforts, and would shrink in proportion as these efforts were impeded. If, then, the claims which socialists put forward on behalf of labour are really to be based, as the earlier socialists based them, on the ground that production alone gives a valid right to possession, labour to-day, instead of getting less than its due, is, if we take it in the aggregate, getting incomparably more, and justice in that case would require that the vast majority of mankind should have its standards of living not raised but lowered.

Is it, then, the reader will here ask, the object of the present volume to suggest that the true course of social reform in the future would be gradually to take away from the majority some portion of what they at present possess, and bind them down, in accordance with the teaching of socialists in the past, to the little maximum which they could produce by their own unaided efforts? The moral of the present volume is the precise reverse of this. Its object is not to suggest that they should possess no more than they produce. It is to place their claim to a certain surplus not produced by themselves on a true instead of a fantastic basis.

Socialists seek to base the claim in question, alternately and sometimes simultaneously, on two grounds--one moral, the other practical--which are alike futile and fallacious, and are also incompatible with each other. The former consists of the a priori moral doctrine that every one has a right to what he produces, and consequently to no more. The latter consists of an assumption that those who produce most will, in deference to a standard of right of a wholly different kind, surrender their own products to those who produce least. The practical assumption is childish; and the abstract moral doctrine can only lead to a conclusion the opposite of that which those who appeal to it desire. But the claim in question may, when reduced to reasonable proportions, be defended on grounds both moral and practical, nevertheless, and the present volume aims at rendering these intelligible. Let us return for a moment to Rousseau and his theory of the social contract. We know to-day that never in the entire history of mankind did any such conscious contract as Rousseau imagined take place; but it is nevertheless true that virtually, and by ultimate implication, something like a contract or bargain underlies the relation between classes in all states of society.

When one man contracts to sell a horse for a certain price, and another man to pay that price for it, the price in question is agreed to because the buyer says to himself on the one hand, "If I do not consent to pay so much, I shall lose the horse, which is to me worth more than the money"; and the seller says to himself on the other hand, "If I do not consent to accept so little, I shall lose the money, which is to me worth more than the horse." Each bases his argument on a conscious or subconscious reference to the situation which will arise if the bargain is not concluded. Similarly, when any nation submits to a foreign rule, and forbears to revolt though it feels that rule distasteful, it forbears because, either consciously or subconsciously, it feels that the existing situation, whatever its drawbacks, is preferable to that which would arise from any violent attempt to change it. The same thing holds good of the labouring classes as a whole, as related to those classes who, in the modern world, direct them. By implication, if not consciously, they are partners to a certain bargain. They are not partners to a bargain because they consent to labour, for there is no bargaining with necessity; and they would have to labour in any case, if they wished to remain alive. They are partners to a bargain because they consent to labour under the direction of other people. It is true that, as regards the present and the near future, they are confronted by necessity even here. This is obviously true of countries such as Great Britain, in which, if the labour of the many were not elaborately organised by the few, three-fourths of the present population would be unable to obtain bread. Nevertheless, if we take a wider view of affairs, and consider what, without violating possibility, might conceivably take place in the course of a few disastrous centuries, the mass of modern labourers might gradually secede from the position which they at present occupy, and, spreading themselves in families or small industrial groups over the vast agricultural areas which still remain unoccupied, might keep themselves alive by labouring under their own direction, as men have done in earlier ages, and as savages do still. They would have, on the whole, to labour far harder than they do now, and to labour for a reward which, on the whole, would be incomparably less than that which is attainable to-day by all labour except the lowest. Moreover, their condition would have all the "instability" which, as Spencer rightly says, is inseparable from "the homogeneous." It could not last. Still, while it lasted, they could live; and, in theory, at all events, the mass of the human race must be recognised as capable of keeping themselves alive by the labour of pairs of hands which, in each case, are undirected by any intelligence superior to, or other than, the labourer's own. In theory, at all events, therefore, this self-supporting multitude would be capable of choosing whether they would continue in this condition of industrial autonomy, with all its hardships, its scant results, and its unceasing toil, or would submit their labour to the guidance of a minority more capable than themselves. Such being the case, then, if by submitting themselves to the guidance of others they were to get nothing more than they could produce when left to their own devices, they would, in surrendering their autonomy, be giving something for nothing--a transaction which could not be voluntary, and would be not the less unjust because, as all history shows us, they would be ultimately unable to resist it. Justice demands that a surrender of one kind, made by one party, should be paid for by a corresponding surrender of another kind, made by the other party; which last can only take the form of a concession to labour, as a right, of some portion of a product which labour does not produce. Labour can, on grounds of general moral justice, claim this as compensation for acquiescence, even though the acquiescence may, as a matter of fact, be involuntary.

Human nature, however, being what it is, these purely moral considerations would probably have little significance if they were not reinforced by others of a more immediately practical kind. Let us now turn to these. The motive which prompts labour to demand more than it produces is itself primarily not moral, but practical, and is so obvious as to need no comment. What concerns us here is the practical, as distinct from any moral, motive, which must, when the situation is understood, make ability anxious to concede it. For argument's sake we must assume that the great producers of wealth are men who have no other motive ultimately than ambition for themselves and their families, and would allow nothing of what they produce to be taken from them by any other human being except under the pressure of some incidental necessity. There is one broad feature, however, which even men such as these understand--the fact, namely, that for successful wealth production one of the most essential conditions is a condition of social stability, or a general acquiescence, at all events, in the broad features of the industrial system, by means of which the production in question takes place. But if the labourers have no stake in the surplus for the production of which such a system is requisite, it may be perfectly true that by escaping from it they would on the whole be no better off than they are, yet there is no reason which can be brought home to their own minds why they should not seek to disturb it as often and as recklessly as they can. There is, at best, no structural connection, but only a fractional one, between their own welfare and the welfare of those who direct them; and a structural connection between the two--a dovetailing of the one into the other--is what ability, no matter how selfish, is in its own interests concerned before all things to secure. In other words, it is concerned in its own interests so to arrange matters that the share of its own products which is made over to the labourers shall be large enough, and obvious enough, and sufficiently free from accessory disadvantages, to be appreciated by the labourers themselves; and the ideal state of social equilibrium would be reached when this share was such that any further augmentation of it would enfeeble the action of ability by depriving it of its necessary stimulus, and, by thus diminishing the amount of the total product, would make the share of the labourers less than it was before.

Though an ideal equilibrium of this kind may be never attainable absolutely, it is a condition to which practical wisdom may be always making approximations; but in order that it may be an equilibrium in fact as well as in theory, one thing further is necessary--namely, that both parties should understand clearly the fundamental character of the situation. And here labour has more to learn than ability; or perhaps it may be truer to say that socialism has given it more to unlearn. If any exchange takes place between two people, which by anybody who knew all the circumstances would be recognised as entirely just, but is not felt to be just by one of the contracting parties, he, though he may assent to the terms because he can get none better, will be as much dissatisfied as he would have been had he been actually overreached by the other. If, for example, he believed himself to be entitled to an estate of which the other was in reality not only the de facto, but also the true legal possessor, and if the other, out of kindness (let us say) towards a distant kinsman, agreed to pay him a pension, he would doubtless accept the pension as a something that was better than nothing; but he would not be satisfied with a part when he conceived himself to be entitled to the whole, and as soon as occasion offered would go to law to obtain it. In other words, if two persons are to make a bargain or contract which can possibly satisfy both, each must start with recognising that the other has some valid right, and what the nature of this right is, to the property or position which is held by him and which is the subject of the projected exchange. Unless this be the case, any exchange that may be effected will, for one of the parties at least, not be a true bargain or contract, but an enforced and temporary compromise. There will be no finality in it, and it will produce no content.

Now, in the case of the bargain or contract between labour and ability, this last situation is precisely that which the teachings of socialism are at present tending to generalise. They are encouraging the representatives of labour to regard the representatives of ability as a class which possesses much, but has no valid right to anything, and with whom in consequence no true bargain is possible; since, whatever this class concedes short of its whole possessions will merely be accepted by labour as a surrender of stolen goods, which merits resentment rather than thanks, because it is only partial.

The intellectual socialists of to-day, and many of their less educated followers, will strenuously deny this. They will declare that they, unlike their predecessors, recognise that directive ability is a true productive agent no less than ordinary labour is; and that able men, no less than the labourers, have rights which they may, if they choose, enforce with equal justice. And if we confine our attention to certain of their theoretical admissions, we need not go further than the pages of the present volume to remind ourselves that for this assertion there are ample, if disjointed, foundations. But the doctrine of modern socialism must be judged, not only by its separate parts, but also by the emphasis with which they are respectively enunciated, and by the mood of mind which, on the whole, it engenders among the majority of those who are affected by it; and, whatever its leading exponents may, on occasion, protest to the contrary, the main practical result which it has thus far produced among the masses has been to foment the impression, which is not the less efficacious because it is not explicitly formulated, that when labour and ability are disputing over their respective rights, ability comes into court with no genuine rights at all; and that, instead of representing (as it does) the knowledge, intellect, and energy to which the whole surplus values of the modern world are due, it represents merely a system of decently legalised theft from an output of wealth which would lose nothing of its amplitude, but would on the contrary still continue to increase were all exceptional energy, knowledge, and intellect deprived of all authority and starved out of existence to-morrow.

So long as such an impression prevails, and indeed until it is definitely superseded by one more in consonance with facts, no satisfactory social policy is practicable. Labour, as opposed to ability, may be compared to a man who believes that his tailor has overcharged him for a coat, and who disputes the account in a law court with a view to its reasonable reduction. In such a case it will be possible for him to obtain justice. The tailor's claim for ?2 may be reduced to a claim for ?0, or ? 5_s._, or ? 15_s._ 6_d._ But if the customer's contention is that he ought to get the coat for nothing, and that he does not in justice owe the tailor anything at all, he is making a demand that no law court could satisfy, and by a gratuitous misconception of his rights is doing all he can to preclude himself from any chance of obtaining them. The mood which socialism foments among the labouring classes is precisely analogous to the mood of such a man as this, and its results are analogous likewise. Its origin, however, being artificial and also obvious in its minutest particulars, the remedy for it, however difficult to apply, is not obscure in its nature. The mood in question results from a definite, a systematic, and an artificially produced misconception of the structure and the main phenomena, good and evil, of society as it exists to-day, and the different parts played by the different classes composing it. It has been the object of the present volume to expose, one after another, the individual fallacies of which this general misconception is the result, not with a view to suggesting that in society as it exists to-day there are no grave evils which a true social policy may alleviate, but with a view to promoting between classes, who are at present in needless antagonism, that sane and sober understanding with regard to their respective positions which alone can form the basis of any sound social policy in the future.

Of the individual demands or proposals now put forward by socialists, many point to objects which are individually desirable and are within limits practicable; but what hinders, more than anything else, any successful attempt to realise them is the fact that they are at present placed in a false setting. They resemble a demand for candles on the part of visitors at an hotel, who would have, if they did not get them, to go to bed in the dark--a demand which would be contested by nobody if it were not that those who made it demanded the candles only as a means of setting fire to the bed-curtains. The demands for old-age pensions, and for government action on behalf of the unemployed, for example, as now put forward in Great Britain, by labour Members who identify the interests of labour with socialism, are demands of this precise kind. The care of the aged, the care of the unwillingly and the discipline of the willingly idle, are among the most important objects to which social statesmanship can address itself; but the doctrines of socialism hinder instead of facilitate the accomplishment of them, because they identify the cure of certain diseased parts of the social organism with a treatment that would be ruinous to the health and ultimately to the life of the whole.

We may, however, look forward to a time, and may do our best to hasten it, when, the fallacies of socialism being discredited and the mischief which they produce having exhausted itself, we may be able to recognise that they have done permanent good as well as temporary evil--partly because their very perverseness and their varying and accumulating absurdities will have compelled men to recognise, and accept as self-evident, the countervailing truths which to many of the sanest thinkers have hitherto remained obscure; and partly because socialism, no matter how false as a theory of society, and no matter how impracticable as a social programme, will have called attention to evils which might otherwise have escaped attention, or been relegated to the class of evils for which no alleviation is possible.

Even to suggest the manner in which these evils would be treated by a sound and scientific statesmanship would be wholly beyond the scope of a volume such as the present, for this reason, if for no other, that, as has been said already, the evils in question are not one but many, each demanding special and separate treatment, just as ophthalmia demands a treatment other than that demanded by whooping-cough. But one general observation may be fitly made, in conclusion, which will apply to all of them. These remedies cannot be included under the heading of any mere general augmentation of the pecuniary reward of labour taken in the aggregate. The portion of the national dividend which goes to labour now, in progressive countries such as Great Britain, Germany, and America, is immensely greater than it was a hundred years ago, and unless industrial progress is arrested its tendency is to rise still further. The main evils to which a scientific statesmanship should address itself arise from the incidental conditions under which this dividend is spent--conditions, largely improvable, which at present deprive it of its full purchasing power. Of this I will give one example--the present structure of great industrial towns. It cannot be doubted that, if the sums now spent on the construction and maintenance of insanitary slums and alleys were employed in a scientific manner, a rent which has now to be paid for accommodation of the most degrading kind would suffice to command, on the strictest business principles, homes superior to those which, if its amount were doubled, would hardly be forthcoming for the labourer in most of our existing streets; while the purchasing power of the existing income of labour would be increased concurrently, and perhaps to a yet greater extent if much of the education, which now has no other effect than of generating impracticable ideas as to the abstract rights of man, were devoted to developing in men and women alike a greater mastery of the mere arts of household management.

But in merely mentioning these subjects I am transgressing my proper limits. I mention them only with a view to reminding the reader once more that the object of this volume is not to suggest, or supply arguments for maintaining that existing conditions are perfect, or that socialists are visionaries in declaring that they are capable of improvement. Its object has been to expose that radical misconception of facts which renders demands visionary that would not be visionary otherwise, and to stimulate all sane and statesmanlike reformers by helping them to see, and also to explain to others, that the improved conditions which socialism blindly clamours for are practicable only in proportion as they are dissociated from the theories of socialism.

FOOTNOTES:

[31] Like all generalisation dealing with complex matters, this must be qualified by individual exceptions. For example, men who have made fortunes for themselves, and have added to the world's stock, by work in the gold-fields, have been in many cases labourers, directing their own efforts by their own intelligence. But some men have been exceptional in one or other of two ways--either in propinquity to the scene of action, or (and this is the more common case) in handihood, determination, and courage. It is not every one who has it in him to go in search of gold to Alaska.

www.ingramcontent.com/pod-product-compliance
Lightning Source LLC
Chambersburg PA
CBHW070354290526
45790CB00004B/1483